THE FIRST RESURRECTION
The Only Resurrection

Flossie Jackson Spencer

WestBow
PRESS
A DIVISION OF THOMAS NELSON

WestBow Press books may be ordered through booksellers or by contacting:

WestBow Press
A Division of Thomas Nelson
1663 Liberty Drive
Bloomington, IN 47403
www.westbowpress.com
1-(866) 928-1240

ISBN: 978-1-4908-0326-5 (sc)
ISBN: 978-1-4908-0327-2 (hc)
ISBN: 978-1-4908-0325-8 (e)

Library of Congress Control Number: 2013913592

Printed in the United States of America.

WestBow Press rev. date: 8/27/2013

The first is the only resurrection whereby we must be saved.

TABLE OF CONTENTS

INTRODUCTION

IN AD 70, JERUSALEM fell and lay in rubble. The temple and Law were destroyed with her, but from her ashes, grace arose, and with it, the beginnings of New Jerusalem.

Will there be a coming rapture, a great tribulation, and a millennial kingdom before the believers of earth can enter heaven? Some believe yes, others no, and still others are undecided. Perhaps you fit in somewhere with these undecided believers. So did I—until God revealed the whole picture from beginning to end to me. Now I will attempt to do the same for you.

The premillennial teaching on the rapture, great tribulation, and millennium are amazingly true, just in the wrong place and time frame, which I will attempt to put in perspective.

Acknowledgments

I OFFER MY THANKS first to God the Father, above all others, whose Son Jesus paid the sin debt for me so I could be restored back to Him through the inspiration of the Scriptures taught to me by the Holy Ghost, making me a resurrected believer.

I would also like to thank His servant, the Reverend Thomas W. Hardy, the Holy Ghost–filled pastor of the Community Baptist Church in Ridgeway, Virginia, where I was raised and converted, for his straightforward teachings that kept me on the wheel, making me a vessel of honor unto the Lord Jesus, whose I am.

I also extend my thanks the Reverend Edgar Pigg, pastor of the Independent Church of God in Ferrum, Virginia, where I learned the doctrines of the end days as believed by most churches today.

Thanks to my precious father and mother, who kept me in church during my childhood.

And lastly, I would like to acknowledge the Reverend Ford Phillips, whose walk with God made me know without a shadow of doubt that there is a God in heaven as well as in the hearts of all believers, for his precious nuggets that I gleaned every time he worked the fields for believers.

PREFACE

AS YOU READ THIS preface and the first three chapters of this book, you will get to know me, my trials, my failures and triumphs, my struggles with the Scriptures and my critics without a word of encouragement but with many of discouragement, and my call into the ministry when I was awakened in the night with a Scripture I actually could see, John. 2:5, and the task of forerunning this doctrine.

Many well-meaning men and women tried to assist me in my walk with God and the study of the Scriptures, but I got somewhat dismayed when they insisted I did not know what I was talking about on the subject of the end times. One such disagreement arose against my belief that the saints from the Old Testament days rose with Christ when He defeated death, which I call the first resurrection, and that we too are part of that same resurrection. Those saints who were in their graves, saved by the Law, are with him now but our resurrection takes place the moment we convert.

One minister's rebuttal was that the saints could not have risen, because the Law cannot save, only the blood. (This is true—the Law quelled the sin that causes death with blood sacrifices, making those who honored those yearly sacrifices sinless.) The minister asserted that the Old Testament saints must wait until we are taken from this world in the rapture before they can ascend.

What? How can they ascend in the second coming if they couldn't in the first? Isn't it recorded in Matthew 27:28 that the graves were opened and the saints came forth? Well, now! If these weren't law-abiding Israelites, who were they? And are we to believe they went back to the grave and not with Christ? Well, duh! If they could not be kept by the *blood* sacrifices while obeying the Law or rise with Christ when He first rose—if the Law did not save them—how could they rise with us in the rapture? (Sometimes I wonder if my critics hear what they tell me.) Did Christ not live and walk according to the Law? Was not his blood shed on Calvary during the days of the Law? Was it not the Law that put Him to death? Did he not rise during the Law days?

Think about that for a moment! We were all—present, past, and future—lifted from death's grip: every soul, at one time, in the twinkling of an eye, when Christ after His death on the cross took the throne to rule over the kingdom of God. His first official act as King was to abolish the Law and institute grace, which occurred fully when the Romans sacked Jerusalem in AD 70. His final act will be to destroy the last enemy, physical death, when the last soul to be saved on earth believes and accepts His work, but we can defeat death now through Christ Jesus. We are, at the instant saved, resurrected from death and forever changed, defeating death! Death has no hold on those who believe. Isn't that great? We become new creatures and take on the nature of Jesus when we accept him as Savior, without sin, and death has no sway over our bodies. Everything has been done except the believing, which is all we have to do to earn eternal life. In my opinion, theologies are not always what they are cracked up to be, and when I was told that my knowledge of the Scripture was not correct, I was somewhat disappointed, but not despairing.

When I first decided to follow God, a special anointing was placed over my life. I knew the walk I would take with God was on the new frontiers, where no one had gone before—not since the reformation days, anyway. I, like countless others who were and are forerunners, offered up excuses covering all the reasons to escape from this task. *That is what excuses are: escape routes.* As I explained to God, first, I am a woman (as if He was not aware of my gender). Certain circles do not accept women in the ministry and surely would not accept this new doctrine at all, let alone from a woman. (I thus had two strikes against me already.) These circles would put me out of every church I teach this truth in, and nowhere will I find peace of mind. (The flesh really does worry about itself.)

"Who said anything about churches?" He questioned. Do you know how He answers our questions with His own? He answered me this: "Did they not kill me when I preached the truth?" End of argument!

Like Paul, I had to die to the flesh, and I had some counting to do. The cost could be great, but would the souls helped be greater than my fear? Yes, I reasoned, because fear stops us from doing what God appoints us to do, causing rebellion. My first move was to build faith in God's call for my life, while the next was to study and grow confident in what He was teaching me concerning His Word—which is, by the way, the only thing that will stand forever, Isaiah 40:8. So, I concluded, if the Word stands, and I stand on the Word, what can cause me to fail? Only fear, I reasoned—so I had to die to the flesh before I started.

CHAPTER 1

First Childhood Lessons

MY MOTHER WAS OF the Primitive Baptist faith, which was the foundation of the Christian doctrine taught to my siblings and me since my father wasn't saved at that time. I never knew my father's view of doctrine, and I suppose I never will, since he died a few years after his conversion. But I know it was different from my mother's, which I called amazing grace because she believed that if one was once saved, one was always saved. It's not that she was riotous or evil, but she never said grace at meals or taught us the oracles, the spoken words of God. She just taught us the right or wrong of everyday life. Some in that faith believes they are punished here for wrongdoings, and with that punishment, they are okay, salvation-wise (once saved, always saved). Her salvation teachings covered us, her offspring, so she was not worried about our souls. That part of sanctification is true to a degree, but we are not in the home of our parents forever. (More about sanctification later.)

When my father converted, we became a family of churchgoers. That was the biggest difference in my parents' salvation: we attended a

Southern Baptist church in my Virginia hometown every Sunday and Wednesday after his conversion. He prayed, said grace, and told us about Jesus.

Being in the construction battalion in World War II caused him to drink, smoke, and curse like the sailor he was. After his conversion, he quit all that. His conversion, coupled with an incident at the Baptist church where we attended Sunday school and church, brought about my salvation. Both his and Mama's faith steered me to where I am today, and I am thankful for that.

The incident at church involved a bee, a pastor, and a hot summer day. Through it, I learned about the Holy Ghost and His power and have never forgotten it. You have no doubt heard about the mule and rooster God used to display His power. Well, now we can add a bee—a hornet, to be accurate. This intruder came in through an open church window. Which one? I have not a clue. They were all open! This life-changing event occurred before air conditioners became popular, so the trespasser took his choice of open windows. I, as well as other congregants, did not realize it was in the church until the pastor asked why the congregation was watching that bee. That "bee" was what we Southerners call a Japanese hornet. I was only nine years old at the time, and the creature seemed huge to me. Naturally, my eyes found and began watching it fly hazardously up and down like a june bug on a string. It flew up against the ceiling, bounced off, dove toward the congregation, and shot back up toward the ceiling. I suppose every eye in the church was on it by then, thanks to the pastor's announcement. Heads were keeping rhythm like apples bobbing in tubs at Halloween.

To regain our attention, the pastor pounded the bookstand with a clenched left fist, annoyed, and asked, "Why is everybody watching that bee? Do you not know the Holy Ghost can bring that creature right down here to this book stand so I can kill it with this book?" He shook a church hymnal above his head. Then the most amazing thing happened. That bee committed suicide. It flew straight down to the bookstand and sat on the spot the pastor had pounded seconds before. He raised the book and killed the enemy. Wow!

That power was awesome. And that same power pulled me to the altar some time later. I could not sit in my pew. It was as if someone had me by the arms, which were straight out in front of me, pulling me. I was actually led to the altar.

I have many fond memories of those days and the messages the pastor brought forth. I praise God for my parents' influence on me, but the pastor's power was the most unusual thing I ever witnessed. He had a profound effect on my life, and I never forgot the lessons I learned as a child—lessons the pastor preached about the Holy Ghost, His power, King Jesus seated on His throne, and God the Father. I learned that one day, through the physical death of our bodies or the second coming of that King, the world would end, and we would all be taken to be with Christ forever, never to be separated from Him again. There were no teachings about future armies surrounding Jerusalem, the great tribulation, or the crowning of the Antichrist, who will rule the world. We were taught that Jesus is now seated on the throne, that the world is His realm, and that we are His people. He appoints earthly rulers to govern us, and they will answer to Him for disobedience and insubordination.

CHAPTER 2

———⋘⋙———

Grown-Up Lessons

I MARRIED A HEATHEN, according to Scripture, and our marriage was not condoned by Christian standards. But if I had known that, I would have rebelled and married him anyway. I did not know it then, but he did not believe in God. Nor would he attend church. I had no license to drive at that time, so I had to stop attending also. Church became a thing of the past, and so did God. I would be thirty-one with four children before I remembered who He was and how badly I needed Him.

After my return to God, I suppose it was to be expected that I go back to the Baptist churches, since I was raised attending them. But my childhood God was not at any of the ones I tried. The congregations were subdued, quiet, and not even one *amen* could be heard from any parishioner. So I had a talk with God and told Him there had to be more to salvation than what I now had. I knew I had fallen away once, and I meant to stay with Him now. I concluded there just had to be

5

more. I did not realize my flesh was weak and that I had everything I needed to overcome my circumstances.

He directed me to a holiness church not far from my home. The worship there was what I was used to—lively and with talk about the Holy Ghost and His baptism. The baptism was news to me, but I recognized His name. When the pastor at this holiness church said we could have the power of the Holy Ghost, I did not understand that doctrine but remembered the power of the Baptist minister, so I believed it. An invitation was given one Sunday night to receive the baptism of the Holy Ghost, so several people, myself included, gathered at the altar. The peace I felt was awesome! If a bomb had gone off in the church I do not think it would have bothered any of us, least of all me.

Two received what I believed to be the baptism that night. I didn't, but that same night, a bright light awakened me in my bedroom. I saw a spiral-shaped object whirling in the air above my head. I watched as it came closer and felt it enter my head and twirl through my body before exiting through my feet. I tried to wake up my husband, but I was frozen. For a while, I could not move or speak. The next thing I knew, it was morning, and I told my husband about my experience.

For the next three days, I felt as if I was glowing. Each time I passed a mirror in our home, I looked to see if I was. That was the most wonderful thing that has ever happened to me, and I have never been the same. I do not know if this event was the baptism or just total surrender, but I knew I was accepted, and the peace I felt confirmed it.

About one year after the baptism experience, still attending the little Holiness Church, where I learned I could have as much of God as I wanted, I heard a word that threw me for a spiritual flip. I thought I could never develop any further in my newfound faith, because I began looking up Scripture about this strange phenomenon every waking minute of free time. The word was *rapture*, and the adventure of my spiritual life began that day.

I believe everything I learned from others and the Scripture since childhood was a divine plan for my life, even before I knew there was a savior named Jesus. Those amazing things I remember from my childhood, plus Mama's and Daddy's faiths, mapped a path I would travel to get to where I am with God right now, however hard the journey might become.

CHAPTER 3

———⟡———

Agony in the Scriptures

IN CHURCH ONE SUNDAY morning approximately a year into my newfound faith, I listened intently as the pastor brought the morning message. I wanted to know everything I could about God. *Hunger* was not the word for it; I was starving. The message that day was about the end of time, taken from 1 Corinthians 15. It concerned the church and tribulation and told of how we would be secretly taken out of this world in the rapture when Christ comes for His bride. All those not ready to go would be left behind and tormented by Satan for seven years as he let loose his fury on the world in the great tribulation. I was dumb about these mysteries of the Scripture, and I was about to embark on a learning experience that has caused many to consider me deceived.

Now, I did not know what the pastor was talking about. During my years in the Baptist church as a youngster, I never heard the words *rapture* or *great tribulation*. My childhood minister said Christ would come for His bride, but not in a secret rapture. Neither would He leave any behind for the Devil to destroy. He said a lake of fire was where the

9

unsaved would go. Well, now I was thoroughly confused, so I looked for the word *rapture* in the Bible. Alas, it was not there, but I did find *great tribulation*. But by the time I painstakingly read enough to amaze me, the holiness pastor said another mouthful of Greek about a thousand-year kingdom called the millennium. Oh my!

In this event, the pastor said, God would bind Satan in a bottomless pit for a thousand years, during which time Christ would take control of all the earth and establish an iron rule. Iron rule? During this iron rule, the millennium, Christ will govern a city brought down from God out of heaven in which He, the now glorified rapture saints, and the surviving humans from the great tribulation will dwell in peace together for one thousand years under His iron rule. Peace under an iron rule! Then, at the end of the millennium, Satan will be let loose to gather an army from the inhabitants of the city in an attempt to destroy New Jerusalem, Christ, and his followers once more.

Another search of the Scriptures commenced, and like *rapture*, the word *millennium* was nowhere to be found. I had never heard anything like those two words, nor the messages associated with them.

One troubling fact about these doctrines is that those not ready to go with Christ in the rapture will be left behind to face the great tribulation and Satan for seven years. Afterward, Satan will be bound for one thousand years. All who make it through these seven years will join Jesus still in fleshly bodies and live in the millennium under the iron rule of Christ. Then, when Christ defeats Satan yet another time after the millennium, all those who endured the great tribulation and were not deceived to help Satan fight Christ after his release from the bottomless pit will enter heaven as saints and live forever.

My heart and mind were in misery. I studied and prayed so hard to find the truth of this new doctrine I was hearing. I was scared that I might never know the truth of it all. Then, on top of my fear, I started having nightmares about the rapture. In these dreams, I would start rising at the sound of the trumpet, and while in the air I would start looking for my children—and because I looked for them, I would fall back to earth. Then, in another dream, at the sound of the trumpet, the earth would split down the center from pole to pole. All who could make it to the right side of the fracture before it became too wide would go with Jesus. Before I awoke, my fingers would be gripping the right edge, my body dangling into the cleft. These dreams went on for months. I knew I had to find the truth of it all, and by studying, I did find a few facts to settle my heart and stop the dreams, at least for a while.

I discovered in the book of Revelation a few things I would like to point out in the next chapter, because these Scriptures took me into a more intense study and a closer look at the reign of Christ. I will begin with two chapters on the questions that kept me studying—questions I hope will keep you reading about what I have learned, one of which is the title of the next chapter.

CHAPTER 4

—◦◦◦◦—

Who Survives to Enter a Millennium?

HAVE YOU REALLY READ the book of Revelation? Have you? If so, do you remember chapters thirteen and nineteen? There are a few things we need to look at together for a minute or two. First, we will look at Revelation 13:7–8,15–16 .

> And it was given unto him to make war with the saints and to overcome them: and power was given him over all kindreds, and tongues, and nations. *And all that dwell upon the earth shall worship him, whose names are not written in the book of life of the Lamb slain from the foundation of the world.* And he had power to give life unto the image of the beast, that the image of the beast should both speak, *and cause as many as would not worship the image of the beast should be killed. And he causeth* all, both small and great, rich and poor, free

and bond, to receive a mark in their right hand or in their forehead.

Now look at Revelation 19:19–21.

> And I saw the beast, and the kings of the earth, and their armies, gathered together to make war against him that sat on the horse, and against his army. And the beast was taken, and with him the false prophet that wrought miracles before him, with which he deceived them that had received the mark of the beast, and them that worshipped his image. These both were cast alive into the lake of fire burning with brimstone. *And the remnant was slain with the sword of him that sat upon the horse,* which sword proceeded out of his mouth: and all the fowls were filled with their flesh.

These were the Scriptures that made me look more closely at this rapture phenomenon, and my first questions were these. If the saved left behind after the rapture were overcome and took the mark of the beast and/or were killed in chapter thirteen if they did not take the mark, and if all those who took the mark were overcome and killed in chapter nineteen—who was left alive to enter this holy city for Christ to rule over with His rod of iron? Even after all this, we have some scholars who declare the following concerning the millennial kingdom.

After the one thousand years are expired, God will release Satan to gather an army from among the city dwellers to fight against the saints and those of the rapture (already immortal) yet another time. I thought the reason for the rapture was to keep Satan from destroying the saints. Are you as confused as I was? I hope so!

I studied the Scriptures day and night as time allowed. After all, I had a husband, four children, and a home to maintain. I did not want to be slothful, but sometimes during my studies, time would escape me, and the children coming in from school would startle me.

I needed help, but where could I go? Everyone I tried to speak to about this subject called me deceived. Who could I talk to? I heard about a shop in town that sold Christian literature, so one day after the kids were off to school and I finished my housework, I drove down and browsed. I found several books about the end times, rapture, and the millennium, bought them all, and returned home to learn the secrets of the end of the world, reasoning with their authors. After a while I began to get frustrated, because none of them agreed. Well, they did agree on a couple of things. You guessed it! They all believed the rapture and the millennium would take place, but they differed on the how and when. The more I read, the more bewildered I became. I got to the point of facing sleepless nights—and, worse than that, those crazy nightmares again!

In these dreams, I would hear the trumpet sound and then see the saints rise, me included, but again, I would start looking for my family, and as soon as I did, I would fall back to the earth. I dreamed I was running from some terrible evil force chasing me and became so out of breath and tired of running. I saw a building and ran into it. It was so dark and cold. I felt a curtain and got behind it and pulled my arms up to my chest to quiet my hard breathing, and in doing so, I looked down toward the floor. I saw my reflection, and I knew that if I could see it, they, whoever they were, could see it too. I turned to run again and bumped into a hand truck, like those used in factories for transporting items to certain departments, and realized I was seeing actual images now. On these hand trucks were hundreds of human bodies, all dressed in white, piled on top of one another! Satan used these to sell as food to the ones taking the mark, hence the buying and selling. It was horrible! These same dreams went on for several years, and all the while, I was still searching the Scriptures for the truth of it all. The books I bought gave me no answers, and one day, in frustration, I got up from the kitchen table where I did my studying, leaving my Bible and all the other books spread across it, threw my hands in the air, and cried out to God, "There has to be one, simple truth!"

Jesus spoke to me as you would and said, "There is." "Read what saith the Lord, not what saith man."

I put the books away and started reading what God said about the end of time. What I have learned will astound you, and my prayer is that you too will seek God regarding what you read hereafter. May He guide you into the truth of His Holy Word.

CHAPTER 5

———❧❧❧———

New Lessons: Back to the Beginning

ADAM IN THE GARDEN: Paradise, grace, and the fall of man.

From Adam to Moses: Satan's spirit was free.

From Moses to Christ: the Law bound Satan's spirit.

From Christ to end of Gentile dispensation AD 70: the Law was fulfilled, Christ was killed and resurrected, the graves were opened, Satan was loosed for the little season, the apostles were ordained, and grace was preached by the Jewish apostles during the little season. Jerusalem was destroyed and Satan cast out, and the New Jerusalem, which is the chosen bride of Christ, the reign of Christ, and the end of earthly rule.

What does all this mean?

There will be no future rapture, great tribulation, Antichrist, or future millennium as taught! What will occur, then, you wonder? Keep reading, and you shall know.

DID YOU KNOW?

DID YOU KNOW THAT **the highest order of angels is the cherubim? They guard the throne of God, they guarded the Ark of the Covenant, and they guarded the garden pair. Their job is to guard, not destroy. One third fell from heaven! Satan was a cherub, a guardian angel.**

The humans in the garden had an encounter with the serpent of the garden, a snake named Lucifer, whom God sent to watch over them and teach them the way of holiness. God has always sent angels to watch over his creation, and Lucifer was perfect until he got a taste of being the god of the earth. Maybe he liked the attention of the humans he communed with, but at any rate, he became lifted up in pride and wanted to be the God. But he had a problem: Adam. (More on the angel Lucifer near the end of this chapter.)

Do you understand what Satan did to deceive Eve? Did she not know that Adam was already as a god? No, she did not. Adam was to teach his wife about creation, God, and worship, just as men are called to do today. He was, after all, the son of God, the ruler of all the earth, just like Christ, his brother, is now.

Satan planted something in the garden of Eden that fateful day too—ideas in the head of the woman: the notion that God was not truthful and that *she* and Adam could be as gods, knowing good and evil, Genesis 3:5. Well, who would not want to be a god? All she and Adam had to do was eat the fruit that God told him they could not eat, right? Wrong! Two sins were committed that day. Some people believe the first sin ever committed was eating the forbidden fruit that caused the sin of rebellion. But the first mistake Adam made was listening to the voice that told him it was all right to eat from the forbidden tree. So his first sin was not that he ate the forbidden fruit, which confirmed his sin of disobedience to God, making his heart ashamed and fearful and guilty. His great first sin was that he obeyed another's voice: Eve's.

Satan's plan could only work with Eve's assistance, so he improvised in her mind the stinginess of God so she would eat the fruit. Satan's desire was to be above God, not equal to Him as he told Eve she and

Adam could be. Satan thought he could overthrow God through man, but God was still Adam's creator, something I believe Satan did not understand. The rule of earth was given to Adam, and by overthrowing him, Satan became the prince of the air—or earth, as Adam was—but the creation still belonged to God. So Satan did not win heaven, just the dust of the earth, or the people. This was how Adam became Satan's problem.

Adam communicated with Lucifer (God's voice) even before Eve was created (Genesis 2), and he would not listen if that same voice said he could now eat the fruit of the Tree of Knowledge of Good and Evil, because he knew the cherub sent from God had already told him he could not eat from that specific tree at any time. So Satan talked with Eve, and she listened to his voice, a voice other than that of her head, Adam, and he in turn listened to her voice, a voice other than God's.

It is not God's job to be the woman's head. He is man's head, and man is woman's head, because man and woman are supposed to be one, with a singleness of heart. Lucifer spoke the words of life to Adam, allowing Adam to notice that something was amiss if he was given a contradictory command. Lucifer spoke with the man, not the woman, as he was directed by God to do. In Scripture, when God spoke to a man or woman, an angel was sent to convey the command. Eve did not hear the words spoken to her husband by the angel. Her knowledge came from her husband, but she knew the guardian and trusted him.

In the New Testament we have clear instructions as to who should be the head of the household.

> Let the woman learn in silence with all subjection. But I
> suffer not a woman to teach, nor to usurp authority over
> a man, but to be in silence. For Adam was first formed,
> then Eve. (1 Timothy 2:11–13)

She is third in the creation order and is thus under man, who is in turn under God.

Eve listened to the idea planted in her mind and was still living after she touched the fruit, so together she and Adam believed the lie. However, the moment the fruit touched Adam's teeth, they both died, because she, like all living human beings, except Jesus, came from Adam. She only had life through her husband, a picture of our life-giving husband, Christ, just as Noah's family lived because of his righteousness during the flood. Eve listened to a voice other than that of her husband, or head (Genesis 3:17). That was Satan's plan all along—to cause man to listen to the voice of another and obey it—and because Adam obeyed the voice of another, man became a servant of a different kind. He did not become the god he was led to believe he would become. His flesh became his god, dominated by the angel Lucifer, destroying the race of man. Sin began with Adam, now separated from God, and because of disobedience, he fell under Satan's power of deception.

When Adam fell, grace was lost. The ruler of the earth, Adam, lost his grace, turning his heart and us with it over to its new king, Satan. Satan wreaked havoc until he destroyed the first world (meaning the earth's people, not the planet). It took him a few years because God's spirit was still inside of man, but he did it. He was not, however, the appointed ruler, for he does not know how to rule. Rule is ordained and given to certain men by God. Satan is not ordained to rule, just to watch, the guardian aspect of his creation. He still has the mentality he fell with—that of a destroyer, a predator, and a stalker without a heart—and he cannot rule justly. Satan blinds because he is blind, and that is what happened to Adam. He became blind and fell into the ditch, losing sight of his wife, future children, and, most importantly, God. But God did not lose sight of man.

Adam was swindled and lost the human race before he knew what happened. The war was on! Yes, God could have snapped his fingers or spoke a word to destroy Adam, but God was dealing with the new ruler, Satan. Man had to defeat Satan to take the rule or dominion of earth back. God gave that rule to man and had to stand down until the time was fulfilled for earth's final ruler, the last Adam. God did cast the Devil into the lake of fire, but his spirit or nature is inbred in us, making us the children of the Devil, as spoken in the New Testament by Jesus in John 8:44. Man had to win this battle if he were to survive, so man had to defeat Satan. However, God did do something. In Genesis 3, He spoke a few words to the woman that caused hatred to rise between her seed and Satan's seed that would bring about his downfall. And we thought man would do it all. The woman was the deceived one, so there should be a time of reckoning for her. Do you agree?

Before I go further, there is something I would like to show you, something God revealed to me when I asked the same question that you might be asking yourself and God as you read. Was it not a snake that tempted Eve? I too fought with this Scripture concerning the snake. The Scripture in Genesis 3:14 tells us the snake would go on its belly in the dust of the earth. In Micah 7:17 I found my answer.

We are the dust of the earth. We were made from it, and when we die, we shall all return thus. Satan's character is bound in our flesh and, by it, humbled. That does not mean he does not fight, just that he only fights the Christians, to cause them to fight against God and destroy His works. If he can destroy the Christians, he has accomplished his goal, but the binding and loosing are up to us, depending on whether we listen to him or not.

As promised, I'll return now to the subject of the talking snake. I was in a congregation in North Carolina during the Christmas holidays some years ago. The speaker believed all the animals in the garden talked and conversed with Adam and Eve until the fall, and they still could talk on December 24 at midnight (hence a talking serpent). Well, when I heard this, my mind stopped right there as the questions started bombarding it. What made Adam and Eve the supreme beings of God's creation? If God wanted to talk with an animal, why did he create a human animal? Would the dog have been a good candidate? How about the horse, or maybe the cat? Why would God kill one of his talking animals to preserve another? (He did so to make clothes for the human animals [Genesis 3:21]). Did the animals have free reign of the garden while man was limited? Why wasn't a commandment given the animals to stay away from the tree? This, of course, is under the assumption that they all could carry on a conversation. These are a few of the demanding questions I needed answers to.

The only animals in the garden able to talk were the humans. Man was different, a human animal that walked upright and could think and convey his thoughts to another human, to God, or to that upright-walking guardian. *Remember, Adam was the one who named all the other animals that only make the sounds we hear that distinguish them from each other.* The snake was Satan, who has been called a serpent ever since he fell.

How did I come to this knowledge? I was reading in the book of Genesis one day about the troubled mind of Abraham over his brother's son, Lot, as a possible heir, when he saw three men approaching him. The Lord enlightened my mind to stop the questions that stayed there for so long about the talking animals. Even though Lot and Abraham had parted company, Lot was still on the mind of his uncle, just as the questions inspired by one statement stayed on mine. When we need answers, we usually get them, although Lot was not the only issue Abraham faced. Lot was an adopted son, Abraham's brother's son, and before the cities of the plain could be destroyed, God had to warn Abraham, because Lot lived in one of them. So the angels were dispatched to Mamre to converse with Abraham. The first verse should open your eyes, but read on anyway in case you miss what I'm referring to.

> And the <u>Lord</u> appeared unto him in the plains of Mamre: and he sat in the tent door in the heat of the day. And he lifted up his eyes and looked, and lo, three men stood by him: and when he saw them, he ran to meet them from the tent door, and bowed himself toward the ground. (Genesis 18:1–2)

Now notice verses 13–21 especially and the rest of that chapter if you wish. What I want you to notice is that several of these verses begin with the words "the Lord said" (unto Abraham).

The voice of the Lord is his angel or, in the case of earth's presidents, an ambassador—one who is authorized to speak in proxy for another, like the angel of the garden, Lucifer. The voice of God is still present in the world today: yours when you defend the gospel, mine while you read this manuscript, or the voice of any other person God designates when He needs a voice.

Now back to where we left off in chapter three of Genesis and the promise made to the woman—the promise of a Savior coming through her seed to undo what Adam did when he failed to obey God.

CHAPTER 6

—⁂—

From Guardian to Destroyer

DID YOU KNOW?

CHAPTER TWELVE OF REVELATION teaches us about a time when Satan tried to destroy the woman's child. He began with Abel. There is a point to be addressed here before we go further, to show you just one little mystery. What does this section of Scripture have to do with Genesis and Eve? The seed is within the woman. Destroy her seed or child, and there goes the project!

Bear with me until we get through these verses to get to Eve.

> And there appeared a great wonder in heaven; (Heaven translated is air, and sky, Strong's Greek Concordance number 3772) a woman clothed with the sun, and the moon (Jacob) under her feet, and upon her head a crown of twelve stars (the twelve sons of Jacob or tribes): And she being with child cried, travailing in birth, and

pained to be delivered. And there appeared another wonder in heaven; and behold a great red dragon, having seven heads and ten horns, and seven crowns upon his heads (Rome). And his tail drew the third part of the stars of heaven, and did cast them to the earth: and the dragon stood before the woman which was ready to deliver, for to devour her child as soon as it was born. (Revelation 12:1–4)

Um, could it be that the woman knew Satan would try to kill her seed as soon as the child was born? Yes, because God put enmity in her to ward Satan off. Eve now knew who he was and what his plan was to rule, since she did pretty much his bidding. The fight was on, ordained by God, and through replenishing the earth, that seed would surely come.

This is the picture of Eve, the mother of all living people and God's chosen seed bearer, ready to fight against Satan to bring forth the chosen one. This is a picture of Moses' mother guarding her precious infant son, the deliverer of Israel. But mainly, this is a picture of Mary, under Roman rule, when the king ordered that all children less than two years of age be killed. Since his fall, Satan has tried to kill the Promised One. Mary, the mother of Jesus, was his last hope.

The deliverer was first promised to Adam and Eve, but He was to come out of the holy nation of Israel (Jacob's race) through a woman's seed, not yet developed into an embryo by sinful man. A lifelong battle called enmity would be fought between the woman and Satan, the woman representing all of womankind, because of the promise made to the first woman. Since Satan lost that battle at the cross, he now has some believing that God has to bind him before Christ, the promised seed, can establish an earthly kingdom. Do you believe Christ is puny? Do you believe Satan is stronger than Christ? Do you think for one minute that God could bind Satan if he is stronger than God the Son? How, then, can we defeat him if it is impossible for Christ? Read on!

Well, now we will look at the time from Moses to Christ, when God made a way for the Savior to enter the scene and revive fallen man. This great new thing would free Satan for a little season until the fulfillment of time or the end of the world as explained by Jesus in John 12:31.

DID YOU KNOW?

Before and after the flood in Genesis, the world was one in unity and language. After the flood, God confused the language of the people on earth, bringing about a dispersion of tribes. That same phenomenon would bring the nations together again before Christ loosed Satan. It was Pentecost. Acts 2:1–6—read it!

What stopped Satan from destroying the second world? Have you ever thought about it? Well, if you haven't, now is as good a time to start as any. It began with Noah, a type of Adam. God started the new world with the eight souls that were saved from the destruction of the first world. God did not call them men, but souls, living souls, named Adam. They were in fleshly bodies, just like we are when we make the transition from lost to saved. We still occupy these bodies after conversion—the flesh remains the same, while the inside changes. The spirit is what guides the soul and flesh after salvation, restoration.

DID YOU KNOW?

The water divided and gathered together during the creation (the dry land took the water's place) was the same water that drowned the world when God destroyed it. Hence, the divided waters came together again and covered the mountains just as the divided people covered the earth afterward.

The new race started with Noah's three sons, Shem, Ham, and Japheth, who were supposed to resettle and replenish the earth after the flood. All spoke one language when they began doing exactly what God meant for them to do, but the flesh of Adam was still covering their bodies—and the flesh defies God. Thus they decided to stay exactly where they were. The defiance began in chapter eleven of Genesis.

> And the whole earth was of one language, and of one speech. And it came to pass, as they journeyed from the east, that they found a plain in the land of Shinar; and they dwelt there. And they said one to another, Go to, let us make brick, and burn them thoroughly. And they had the brick for stone, and slime they had for mortar. And they said, Go to, let us build a city and a tower, whose top may reach unto heaven; and let us make us a name, lest we be scattered abroad upon the face of the whole earth. (1–4)

The whole earth was not being settled in different regions as God meant it to be, for Noah's sons only moved the borders to meet the demands of population growth. They built only one city, and instead of going outward, they went upward toward heaven. If another flood did occur, they would be safe, high above the waters in the tower. Dispersion came only after God confounded their language, causing some to speak in foreign tongues (Genesis 11:5–8). When the people all spoke in different languages, their environmental project came to a halt. God's plan for us is to reach heaven, but not by our design. The descendants of Noah were altering God's plan, so God stopped it abruptly.

Some people do not understand the mechanics of salvation. They wonder why God allows bad things to happen to humans, including why He allows for sin in the first place. God, however, has never allowed sin. The problem is in man, because God gave dominion over the earth to Adam, and in turn, Adam gave his dominion up to Satan, who was full of sin, which was passed to Adam after his rebellion against God. God could not override the fixed authority that was given to man, and because we defy His desire for us, we cause our own problems. His plan of salvation has been to stop sin, first with the Law of Moses and then with fulfillment by grace through Christ. However, there is pleasure in sin, and anything that brings us pleasure is addictive, making it harder to stop dabbling in it. The idea of being a god gave Adam pleasure. When we entertain sin, it will take us further than we want to go and keep us longer than we want to stay. Adam certainly went further than he thought, and there was no way back.

As long as we are in these bodies of flesh, we are in trouble as far as sin is concerned. The flesh likes pleasure, and according to the Scriptures, there is pleasure in sin for a season (Hebrews 11:25). Everyone in sin enjoys being there. People often blame God for misfortunes or anything else that disrupts human pleasure, not realizing that He is the author of real joy, from whom all blessings flow. Because there was no law and order ordained by God to humans until Moses' day, all men lived in and for pleasure, heading right back down the path of sin to destruction. Without the Law, man would once again be on the brink of extinction, as the cities of the plain indicate. If we had the power to change what brings us pleasure, we could stop the cycle of death. Jesus is the only cycle breaker, and Satan has been trying to kill Him since the promise of His coming was foretold to Eve. However, Satan did not know Christ was supposed to die, for if he had known that, he would not have killed the Lord of glory (1 Corinthians 2; 8).

Moses was the first of many saviors directing us to the Savior. Since law does not bring us pleasure when it is administered to us personally, we hate it, often object to it, and attempt to change it. We even try to change Scripture to fit our lifestyles instead of changing our lifestyles to fit the Scriptures, all in an attempt to enter heaven some way other than salvation—just like the city builders of Genesis 11. All of this proves that we know we need salvation, without which no man may enter the one and only true city, the city of God.

God's plan was still going to be carried out, no matter how difficult man became. Through these defiant earthlings, God would raise up a few to carry out His plan to save us all. Enter the first Hebrew, Abraham, from the dispersed race of Shem, and the first High Sheriff, Moses. By the way, the spirit that was breathed into Adam at his creation was still there and allowed men to overcome before and after the flood, until the Law was drafted and delivered to Moses.

Chapter 7

The Binding of Satan

Did You Know?

LAW IS STRONGER THAN the flesh. The Law put man to death for his transgressions—capital punishment, if you will. Because man could not be put to death for disobedience before the Ten Commandments, he became responsible for his actions after their inception, now able to stop sin, or the power of the flesh, Satan.

Of all the writers in the world, I believe Paul and Martin Luther were two of the greatest. They understood the purpose of the Law. Paul wrote in Galatians 3:19, "Wherefore then serveth the law? It was added because of transgressions, till the seed should come to whom the promise was made, to Adam and Eve; and it was ordained by angels in the hand of a mediator, Moses."

Here is what Martin Luther translates Galatians 3:19 to reveal to us. Law came in to increase sin. It isn't that sins were not committed or did not abound without the Law, but they were not known to be transgressions or sins of such grave consequence. On the contrary, most of them, even the greatest of them, were considered as righteous. Now, when sin is unrecognized, there is no room for a remedy and no hope for a cure, because men will not submit to the touch of a healer when they imagine themselves well and in no need of a physician. Therefore, the Law is necessary to make sin known so that when its gravity and magnitude are recognized, man, who in his pride imagines himself well, may be humbled and may sigh and gasp for the grace that is offered in Christ.[1]

> But before faith came, we were kept, bound, under the law, shut up unto the faith, which afterwards should be revealed. Wherefore the law was our schoolmaster to bring us unto Christ, that we might be justified by faith. But after that faith is come, we are no longer under a schoolmaster. (Galatians 3:23–25)

The schoolmaster was the Law. After Christ came we were released from its grasp into grace, so our flesh would no longer be held captive by its desire to sin. The whole world over is saved by this wonderful work of salvation. All we have to do is believe, and once we do, we are translated into the kingdom of God, born again and free from the sin of our past and future and the spirit of Satan as well.

God could not stop sin until He stopped Satan, literally, so He bound the flesh of man through the Law. God had to expose sin to stop it. Sin was the reason Adam's soul died and was what brought death upon us all. There had to be something stronger than the will of man to bring his flesh under subjection, because man was under the penalty of death with no lawyer or amendments. Death was hereditary, passed on through the blood of fathers to their children at birth as a disease, and there was no cure. Without Law, the generations of Noah would have

---

1   Martin Luther, *The Bondage of the Will* (Grand Rapids: Baker Book House 1976), 346.

kept multiplying until transgressions became just as bad as the world before Noah, when sin drove man to the brink of extinction.

Remember the words God spoke unto Adam? "For in the day that thou eatest thereof thou shalt surely die" (Genesis 2:17).

Guess what we were cured of? "But he was wounded for our transgressions, he was bruised for our iniquities: the chastisement of our peace was upon him; and with his stripes we are healed" (Isaiah 53:5). We were healed of death. Adam ate the forbidden fruit and died! Then he and his descendants were exposed to a life of death. But the medicine to cure humanity's ills was in the form of a small seed in the reproductive system of the woman.

Recall the birth of Moses for a moment while remembering Revelation 12 again and the male child scenario. He, like Christ, was almost murdered as an infant. Earthly nonbiological fathers raised both. Both were brought out of their countries to fight the modern-day religion and rulers. Moses imposed the law of God on the people he brought out of sin just as Christ offers grace to believers when they are brought out. That same system of the Law was in action when Christ came on the scene many years later and is what put Him to death. If we will let our minds remember their earthly lives, we will see that Moses and Jesus shared some striking similarities.

The first step to heal man was for Moses, the first deliverer ordained by God to lead the Israelites out of bondage, to administer the Law in the desert. That nation comprised the descendants of Isaac, who were designated to carry the oracles, the spoken words of God until Christ's death resurrected grace. Egypt was a type of grave, and the Israelites were among the dead in that grave. Their deliverance would be a type of restoration to God, akin to grace from sin through Jesus.

The children of Jacob worked their fingers to the bone for their taskmasters in Egypt and died without inheritance—just like when man in sin obeys Satan's commands and dies without the splendors of eternity with Jesus. Moses was a type of Jesus, delivering God's children from the bondage of the grave, the very captivity Christ led man out of through His death on the cross. People who are in sin are very similar to the Israelites. All who are astray in sin are still in spiritual Egypt, or death. Even after the medicine of Jesus' sacrifice was administered, some died, for they would not receive it. Sounds like some of us today, don't it?

Are you ready to receive what bound Satan? *It was the Law.* Wait! If it was the Law, how can the Millennium be in the future? Maybe you see what I am driving at by now.

DID YOU KNOW?

If the Law bound Satan, then the fulfillment of the Law would release him. The Law stopped or halted death by binding the lust of the flesh to sin. With the flesh restrained, so is Satan! And if grace freed man from the Law, it also freed Satan from the binding of the flesh! There are no more tablets of stone, just grace in a heart of flesh.

Paul knew what the Law meant and why God had to raise a lawgiver—or should I say a law keeper? Here is some of the wisdom of the greatest writer I know of.

> For until the law sin was in the world: but sin is not imputed when there is no law. Nevertheless death reigned from Adam until Moses, even over them that had not sinned after the similitude of Adam's transgression, who is the figure of him that was to come. (Romans 5:13–14)

God raised Moses up to know sin in one of the most godless places in history, Egypt, and he even murdered one of its citizens. Its inhabitants worshipped everything imaginable except the God of heaven. Moses' work was exactly the same as Christ's, and he was the figure of Him who was to come, in that he too brought salvation. Even after his death, the

Law kept and saved God's people, just as grace saves and keeps them today.

Those who were born and died before the Law, (including Adam and Eve), those who died without knowledge of the Law after it was instituted, or even those who had not committed actual sins were not excluded from death—even infants. Death reigned, not life. Original sin is the issue, not innocence. Not sinning after the similitude of Adam meant not disobeying direct commands from God. After the fall of man sent him from the presence of God, there was no voice of God to the people, but there was some kind of law of the land, because the Scripture above mentions "them that had not sinned after the similitude of Adam's transgression." Man's goodness came from his knowledge of God through the spirit God breathed into him at creation, and we are born with that same knowledge today. That is the inner voice that tries to deter us from sin. We are not innocent of the original sin brought on by Adam's transgression, the alien nature that causes us to obey the flesh and sin. It is a character trait, so to speak, that marks us as Adam's sons until conversion, at which time we acquire heavenly traits of the Father by His Son, Jesus.

Let's look at the binding of Satan as revealed to me by the Holy Ghost. Satan has always been reserved for judgment, and both Peter and Jude told us how, why, and where. We will look at the Scriptures of these two men now.

> For if God spared not the angels that sinned, but cast them down to hell, and delivered them into chains of darkness, to be reserved unto judgment. (2 Peter 2:4)

> And the angels, which kept not their first estate, but left their own habitation, he hath reserved in everlasting chains under darkness unto the judgment of that great day. (Jude 6)

No matter how far away Satan may be locked up, his *spirit* is still in this world as long as humans are in their flesh. As a matter of fact, just as Christ said, as long as I am in the world; the world has light, because we have His life, or spirit, in us as Christians. Same application, different mode! Satan's nature was good until he fell, taking with him as many angels as he could persuade to mutiny against God. Through his spirit, he had full sway before the flood, which proves man cannot deliver himself by his own merits. The darkness of the hearts of lost evil men is really where that serpent spirit is, and humans yield themselves to the flesh every day and will continue to do so until Jesus changes hearts and kicks (or casts) him out. Because of the sin that came with disobedience, humans are now in the image of Satan, and thus the flesh is prone to do evil.

Look at a few passages from John. "Now is the judgment of this world: now shall the prince of this world be cast out" (12:31). "Of judgment because the prince of this world is judged (15:1). *World* means people in whose bodies Satan's spirit dwells. This world steeped in sin cannot be the physical earth, but earthly humans, for spirits must have a body to have rest. Remember Matthew's words in chapter twelve?

> When the unclean spirit is gone out of a man, he walketh through dry places, seeking rest, and findeth none. Then he saith I will return into my house from whence I came out; and when he is come he findeth it empty, swept, and garnished. Then he goeth and taketh with him seven more spirits more wicked than himself, and they enter in and dwell there: and the last state of that man is worse than the first. Even so shall it be with this wicked generation. (43–45)

We can be homes to unclean spirits, and many humans are. These spirits steal, kill, and destroy through the humans they occupy, just like their master, and unless God saves the souls of those precious humans, they will all be cast into the lake of fire and brimstone where the beast and false prophet are. So it is not hard to understand that even if Satan is bound in some faraway galaxy, if we are in these bodies of flesh we will still sin until Jesus fills us with his spirit, casting out Satan's. Even then we must fight the good fight of faith to keep pure.

I hope this helps you understand the binding and loosing. In other words, Satan is a part of the human being and still has sway because we are also flesh and carnally minded. The Law bound men's flesh for fear of death, so the Law was stronger than the flesh. Grace, however, binds our hearts and flesh, because grace is stronger than the Law and replaces our stony heart with one of flesh. Grace cast out the satanic nature in our body that holds our soul, because it cast sin out of repentant believers. Our flesh, though, is still carnal, and we can be deceived—when at salvation, Satan's spirit is cast from our bodies, it is then freed to deceive the nations, of God, and the lost. (Revelation 20). But remember, we are bound by a flaming sword (the Word) to keep him out, just as the cherub with the flaming sword kept him out of paradise with the Word of God.

CHAPTER 8

The Curse Broken

DID YOU KNOW?

THE MALE PASSES SIN to the succeeding generations. The male propagates sin by blood, which is why Christ was born sinless even though He was clothed with flesh. The seed was the woman's, fertilized by God, who is sinless. When we are born again, we too become sinless, and the generations that follow are counted righteous if we stay in the covenant.

Adam is the father of all who are dying—in the flesh, that is—but Eve is the mother of all who are living. While Adam was sinless, Eve could have conceived children who were born sinless. Those children could have come from him as spotless as he was when he was created. However, he fell for the device of Satan, plummeting us all into death— the bottomless pit, if you will—without Christ.

Nevertheless death reigned from Adam to Moses, even

over them that had not sinned after the similitude of Adam's transgression, who is the figure of him that was to come…. For if by one man's offense death reigned by one; much more they which receive abundance of grace and of the gift of righteousness shall reign in life by one, Jesus Christ. (Romans 5:14,17)

Did you know?

If Adam had children before he fell, they too would have died the same death he did, for they would have come out of Adam.

Sanctification was a topic in the introduction of this book, and as promised, we will discuss it at length now.

The wonderful account of our sacrifice whereby we were sanctified is recorded in the book of Hebrews.

For it is not possible that the blood of bulls and of goats should take away sins. Wherefore when he cometh into the world, he sayeth, sacrifice and offering thou wouldest not, but a body thou hast prepared me: In burnt offerings and sacrifices for sin thou hast had no pleasure. Then said I, Lo, I come in the volume of the book it is written of me, to do thy will, O God. Above when he said, Sacrifices and offering and burnt offerings and offering for sin thou wouldest not, neither hadst pleasure therein; which are offered by the law; Then said he, Lo I come to do thy will, O God. He taketh away the first, that he may establish the second. By the which will we are sanctified through the offering of the body of Jesus once for all. (10:4–10)

Death came through one man, and grace came through one man. The first Adam bought death; the last Adam bought life. Death came through the bloodline of the man who sinned and through birth passed death to all men. It was through the bloodline of God, passed on to Jesus, that sin stopped at the cross. When we are born again, we are called the children of God, making us as His literal children—sinless. We were adopted into the covenant of grace through sanctification.

God-fearing parents need not worry about their little ones who die at birth or at any age while under their roof, if God knows the parents, He knows the children, and they are holy at birth because their fathers are now holy. The same applies to either saved parent. But those born outside the covenant of grace are as lost as their parents. To understand this more, read 1 Corinthians 7:12–14. We are born holy through the miracle of justification, and so are our children. Through justification, they are saved right along with us, providing we stay married after salvation or even if an unbelieving parent leaves—no matter if children are born before or after our salvation begins. How did it become so? Like this.

You see, God has no sin in Him, so there was no evil to infiltrate the body of His Son as it was transmitted through Adam to his sons. This is the miracle of sanctification. If only one parent is saved, the spouse and children are counted righteous because of the oneness or singleness of the husband and wife. The whole house becomes protected, because the Lamb's blood has been applied. The covenant still works today the same as in the days of the Law. And as long as the covenant exists within families—if the children leave home, marry, and have children with Christ as the center—sanctification will always rule. Even when a prodigal leaves the fold, he will be welcomed home as promised. Know this: God is our heavenly Father with life, and life and sanctification are through Him—not like an earthly father, who is full of death.

Remember when God told Satan in Genesis 3:15: "I will put enmity between thee and the woman, and between thy seed and her seed." This promise made to the woman was how she got even with Satan and is why he tries to kill her seeds. God was referring to Christ as her seed, not Adam's. Christ had to come through the birth canal of a woman to obtain a body of flesh so he could die, and He had to be fertilized by God to be born innocent. Eve's name means "mother of all living" (Genesis 3:20). Maybe now the meaning of her name will stand out in your mind. A woman's seed is sinless until man, Adam's nature, fertilizes it, if you will accept it.

DID YOU KNOW?

Birth is the door to the earth, to the sheepfold, and to heaven. Anyone who enters any other way is an alien. Equated in the Scriptures to a thief and a robber, Satan entered through deception, not the door!

Eve's seed entered the world through the door, which is birth. Satan came in some other way, which is why he is a deceiver. To enter this world rightly, we are born. To enter heaven, we must be born again. If anyone enters any other way, he or she is like a thief and a robber—or like Satan. So God came to Mary through the Holy Ghost, and she conceived. The seed was pure because the male of our species did not fertilize it. The bloodline is a mystery of God, but a beautiful one. That is how Christ entered the world and was born sinless. He was shaped just like us, of flesh and bone through the woman's seed—much like the first Adam except for His blood. He is God's seed and Son through a different bloodline, a sinless bloodline. He was at all points tempted like Adam was to sin, yet He resisted—and we gained life because He did not sin. Had He yielded to Satan as His brother Adam did, we would all be lost and without hope, because God would have died.

Let me try to paint you another picture. The word of God spoke the world—day and night, seas, trees, man, and beast—into existence. The word of God is all power and all knowledge. I believe we are in agreement so far. Now, in the kingdom of God, the Word, John, 1: 1 became a wee seed in the woman, was fertilized to become an embryo, and was born to walk and talk in the person of God the Son. *Christ created the kingdom of God while Satan was devising a way to kill Him, just as it was in Adam's day—which is why God would have died if Christ had sinned. Christ was God in flesh and if his flesh listened to the voice of Satan and obeyed, sin would enter his body and there was not another to die for sin, and that is the only way God could die.)*

When God revealed to me how His Word became blood and bone covered over with flesh, I had a spell you would not believe. These little secrets have let me know that His Spirit does teach us His ways and mysteries.

So now, when we believe in the Son's work of grace, we are at that time born again into the family of God: "Ye are the body of Christ" (1 Corinthians 12:27). And as children of a sinless father, we are counted as sinless babies. The same miracle that birthed Christ delivers us from death to life—the new birth, if you will receive it—making us part of His body.

I want to clarify sin. Sin is only passed through the male of the species. That is correct. You see, Christ came through the female, sinless. The bloodline or sin line is from the male. All children of earthly parents are born in sin because the male blood is contaminated by death. That wee seed in the female is as pure as can be until sperm makes contact with it. When it does, the embryo becomes defiled with sin and death. The woman was deceived, but the man is the one who sinned—and this is why all who are born of man die. Remember, when Adam ate the fruit, both his and Eve's eyes were opened, because she was part of him, made from the rib, and she died the same instant he did. All die because of Adam's disobedience.

God is holy and his blood is undefiled. Christ came through God's genes, making Christ and all who become children by new birth sinless. When we accept Christ's redemptive work, we become born again through the new Adam, which is how our species can now have pure blood by Him whose blood is pure.

We are all, the world over, from Adam and thus were conceived under sin, Jew and Gentile alike. The Jews carried the oracles of God under the old covenant and were His only people, but now the words of life are engraved upon our hearts—no more Law or letter. The new covenant makes us all the same, lost and unsaved, and since Christ rose, the whole of mankind becomes new creatures when they accept the plan of salvation as taught by Him in the Bible. According to Paul in Romans 7:14, "Man is carnal, sold under sin." Adam succumbed to Lucifer because he wanted to be a god. That is what happens when we become selfish: we think only of ourselves and try to become our own deliverers. Who would need God if we could deliver ourselves? Enter the Law.

Why did God, through Moses, decree the Law? Was it to send us to hell? No! Paul said it was our schoolmaster, to teach us about heavenly things, including the Father, Son, and Holy Ghost—to teach us why we were dying and how to stop the curse of death. Jesus was the only human being born sinless. If we were born sinless, as some believe infants are, Jesus did not need to be born—and much less to die.

DID YOU KNOW?

In Genesis 6:3, when God saw the wickedness of man's heart and said, "My spirit shall not always strive with man, for that he is also flesh," He did not mean He would stop working with us or for us, as some believe will occur in the tribulation. He meant that His spirit inside us would be so overcome by our flesh that within 120 years, the spirit of man would no longer be able to control his flesh, and there would be no human left with an inkling of good in him.

Because death reigned, the Law was drafted to expose sin and stop men from dying. It worked, but human bodies were still held captive by death through Satan. Remember, he stole us from God and controls the flesh. Jews could believe in God but could not be united with Him after death because the flesh was held captive in the grave. (Remember spiritual Egypt!) The Law, binding Satan's spirit, was in the world until the kingdom of God was established. Grace could not come until Christ died on the cross, nor could He rise to be the first fruits of them who slept. In other words, humans could not rise until He first rose, and He could not rise until He first died. Satan had no dominion over Christ, because there was no sin in Him. If He had sinned, He would have died, just like Adam.

On the cross he spoke those precious words: "It is finished." All the work needed for our salvation was finished. The official day began when the temple was destroyed, at which time the kingdom of the Jews was moved from the physical Holy Land into the hearts of the believers. All the people of earth were at that time joined together under sin. No longer was there a holy nation in Israel—just lost souls redeemed by the miracle of justification to become the kingdom of God.

> Is the law then against the promises of God? God forbid: for if there had been a law given which could have given life, verily righteousness should have been by the law. But the scripture hath concluded all under sin, that the promise by faith of Jesus Christ might be given to them that believe. But before faith came, we were kept under the law, shut up unto the faith, which should later be revealed. Wherefore the law was our schoolmaster to bring us unto Christ, that by faith we might be justified by faith. But after that faith is come, we are no longer under a schoolmaster. (Galatians 3:21–25)

The promise was to those under the Law. Those who watched for the Messiah saw him—and saw their faith fulfilled as well. Grace frees from the Law and the graves, for when Christ died, the graves were opened, and the saints rose. The body lives again—no need for a grave! They even went to town before they went to heaven. Hey, it is rapture time! Read it!

> And the graves were opened; and many bodies of the saints which slept arose, and came out of the graves

after his resurrection, and went into the holy city, and appeared unto many [all]. (Matthew 27:52–53)

Could that have been the rapture, and could we be "the rest of the dead" mentioned in Revelation 20:5?

I guess there is some more explaining to be done!

CHAPTER 9

The First Resurrection

DID YOU KNOW?

AS FAR AS GOD was concerned, we were all dead. Adam was dead, so we were all born dead. The saints of the Old Testament went to their graves believing that they would not stay there. They died believing in a Savior who would release them after His resurrection. But the rest of the dead—we who remained alive in fleshly bodies after He resurrected the saints—would have to wait for grace before our change from mortal to immortal could take place—hence "the rest of the dead." The resurrection is the raising of the dead before death. The Law perfected the saints of the Old Testament before their physical death. Their bodies were dead, but not their souls. We have immortal souls, but our bodies must wait for the change, all done before we go to the grave.

Christ walked and talked with His followers from his entering the priesthood at age thirty until he died at age thirty-three and a half. In

John 5:25, Jesus makes a profound statement: "Verily, verily, I say unto you, The hour is coming, and *now is*, when the dead shall hear the voice of the Son of God: and they that hear shall live."

Revelation 20:5 states, "But the rest of the dead lived not again until the thousand years were finished. This is the first resurrection."

After Jesus' resurrection, all those preserved by the Law were taken with him to glory. The rest of the "dead in trespasses and sin" (Ephesians 2:1), Jew and Gentile, would have to accept the plan of salvation brought in by grace and delivered by the apostles to be saved and make it to heaven when Christ returns for his bride.

Jesus died for all, but no one was under grace yet, except the apostles, whom Jesus baptized with the Holy Ghost after His resurrection.

> Then said Jesus to them again, Peace be unto you: as my Father hath sent me, even so send I you. And when he had said this, he breathed on them, and saith unto them. Receive ye the Holy Ghost: Whose soever sins ye remit, they are remitted unto them; and whose soever sins ye retain, they are retained. (John 20:21–23)

Christ gave His apostles the words of life, but they had to wait in Jerusalem until the enforcer (i.e., the Holy Ghost) came, which was before Jerusalem's destruction. Once He entered the room, their tongues became afire with the words of life, and the rest of the dead who believed in Jesus began to be alive. The apostles were still under the Law, and they fought the same council that Jesus had fought.

The dead in John 5:25 are not the dead who have died and been buried. They are the dead in trespasses and sins, the living dead, the rest of the dead, such as the Pentecost crowd in the upper room, before the physical death of the body. After we die the physical death, there is another death we must face if we die lost. It is the second death.

> But the fearful, and unbelieving, and the abominable, and whoremongers, and sorcerers, and idolaters, and all

liars, shall have their part in the lake, which burneth with fire and brimstone: which is the second death. (Revelation 21:8)

The dead that Christ speaks of in John 5:25 are those whose souls are dead, like Adam. When we accept Christ's work at Calvary, we die a death then also, to the flesh or world, but our bodies do not die. It is really a reversal of the curse brought about through Adam. He died, but still lived after he ate the fruit. We die to sin and become alive in these physical bodies until the time we die a physical death of the flesh called sleep. The *dead* dead, those who are in the graves, are treated in verses 28 and 29.

Marvel not at this: for the hour is coming in the which all that are in the graves shall hear his voice. And shall come forth; they that have done good, unto the resurrection of life; and they that have done evil, unto the resurrection of damnation.

These lost dead in the grave sleep too, but true death awaits them when they are wakened from the first death.

Only the saints who died abiding in the Law came forth when Christ rose, for death is what kept their flesh in the grave, separated from God. The Law kept death from the Old Testament saints just as grace works for us today. They were only sleeping, for they were obedient to that Law and became part of the first resurrection. The rest in the graves who died under disobedience to the Law are counted among the dead waiting for the second death (John 5:28–29). They will be resurrected by the same trump that raises those who have gone to sleep since Jesus rose, when all shall come forth not in two groupings, but one, to be separated to face their fate. The good will be distinguished from the evil—one resurrection, two classes, one damned and one perfected.

Those who died during the days of the Law and kept it were perfected and will thus not see the second death. They were protected from Satan's nature, their flesh bound tight by the Law of Moses.

> Jesus, when he had cried again with a loud voice, yielded up the ghost. And, behold, the veil of the temple was rent in twain from the top to the bottom; and the earth did quake, and the rocks rent. And the graves were opened, and many bodies of the saints which slept arose, and came out of the graves after his resurrection, and went into the holy city, and appeared unto many [all]. (Matthew 7:50–53)

I submit to you this is the first resurrection and is what Christ talks about in John 5 and also in Revelation 20:5—because the dead (unsaved) cannot live again after the death of the body. (There is no life outside of Christ, only eternal death.) The resurrection is for the body (of Christ, that is), which we are, so you see, the white throne judgment is what separates, the believers from the sinners now.

Jesus makes a statement to Martha upon his arrival after the death of her brother, Lazarus.

> Then when Jesus came, he found that he [Lazarus] had lain in the grave four days already. Now Bethany was nigh unto Jerusalem, about fifteen furlongs off: and many of the Jews came to Martha and Mary, to comfort them concerning their brother. Then Martha, as soon as she heard that Jesus was coming, went and met him: but Mary sat still in the house. Then Martha said unto Jesus, Lord, if thou hadst been here, my brother had not died, But I know, that even now, whatsoever thou wilt ask of God, God will give it thee. Jesus saith unto her, thy brother shall rise again. Martha saith unto him, I know that he shall rise in the resurrection at the last day. Jesus saith unto her, I am the resurrection, and the

life: he that believeth in me, though he were dead, yet shall he live: And whosoever liveth and believeth in me shall never die. Believeth thou this? Now verse 39. Jesus said, Take ye away the stone. Martha, the sister of him that was dead, saith unto him, Lord, by this time he stinketh: for he hath been dead four days. [Then Jesus prayed to the Father.] ... And when he thus had spoken, he cried with a loud voice, Lazarus, come forth. And he that was dead came forth, bound hand and foot with grave clothes: and his face was bound about with a napkin. Jesus saith to them, Loose him and let him go. (John 11:17–25,43–44)

Jesus directs the body, taking away the stony heart, giving the body a heart of flesh, and freeing the body from death. Oh grave, where is thy victory? Martha believed Jesus could heal the body, but to bring one back from the dead was not possible until the last trump.

This is a picture of our resurrection from dead to living while we are yet in these bodies of death. These verses' meanings are twofold. Firstly, Christ has power to raise those who have died the physical death of the flesh and those who die to sin believing in his name. Because Christ came into the world sinless, lived sinless, and died sinless, the grave could not hold him. He then became the first one to rise, causing all who believed in His first coming to rise with him and all who believe in His name today to rise at His second coming, as Martha declares in John 11:27: "She saith unto him, Yea, Lord, I believe that thou art the Christ, the Son of God, which should come into the world." Therefore she knew her brother would rise in the general resurrection at Christ second coming.

Jesus came from and returned to the Father sinless. Because He lives, we live if we believe in His name. That is not much to do to have eternal life, is it?

CHAPTER 10

***

The King of the Earth

CHRIST IS THE KING of earth and glory! He has put down all rule, power, and authority. Daniel, in his book, told us that Christ would establish His kingdom during the reign of earthly kings, not after a one-world ruler as taught in premillennialism. Read it yourself.

> And in the days of these kings shall the God of heaven set up a kingdom, which shall never be destroyed: and the kingdom shall not be let to other people, but it shall break in pieces and consume all these kingdoms, and it shall stand forever. (Daniel 2:44)

Hallelujah.

The book of Daniel declares the kingdom of God would be established during the days of earthly kings, not after they were all destroyed, for this kingdom would be a spiritual kingdom, never destroyed. Nowhere does the Bible tell us that there will be a one-thousand-year kingdom of God that Satan ravishes at its end.

There are three divisions of earthly power mentioned in the Scriptures: the nations of the Israelites, the nations of the Gentiles, and the nation of Christ. Two have fallen, and one now stands.

When Christ was born, the Roman Empire was the ruling power after the fall of the Greeks, whose empire comprised the whole Mediterranean Sea, still under Alexander's influence; his succeeding rulers were called kings of the earth. It was in the midst of these powers that Christ came and died, reclaiming the world when He did.

Jerusalem was under the rule of the Ptolemaic dynasty and then the Seleucids, who divided Alexander's empire after his death. Later, the Hasmonean dynasty, led by a Jewish priest named Mattathias and his sons, fought the Seleucids when Antiochus defiled Jerusalem's temple. Their rebellion was successful until Rome took the empire and Jerusalem with it. The Jews had all but lost their identity—and Hebrew language, since Alexander made Greek the official language of his empire, which included Jerusalem and is why the New Testament is written in Greek; half of the Roman Empire spoke Greek as well.[2]

Satan's agenda was to kill Jesus before He could become the King of Jerusalem. He tried via the slaughter of the innocents, again when tempting Him to jump from the temple, and yet again when He was put on the cross. Satan sure thought he had Him then. But again, Paul had something to say about that:

> But we speak the wisdom of God in a mystery, even the hidden wisdom, which God ordained before the world unto our glory. Which none of the princes of this world knew: for had they known it, they would not have crucified the Lord of glory. (1 Corinthians 2:7–8)

---

2   *The NIV Study Bible* (Grand Rapids: Zondervan, 2011), 1573.

Now see what Luke said about the hidden wisdom of God.

> The kings of the earth [remember the ones referred to by Daniel] stood up, and the rulers were gathered together against the Lord, and against his Christ. For of a truth against thy holy child Jesus, whom thou hast anointed, both Herod, and Pontius Pilate, with the people of Israel, were gathered together, for to do whatsoever thy hand and thy counsel determined before to be done. (Acts 4:26–28)

Seems to me that Satan's agenda played right into God's, did it not?

There have not been kings ruling whole provinces in hundreds of years. When the kings ruled, it was over several nations at one time called empires, considered the whole Earth. We have rulers now, but they are in the forms of governments with presidents. Christ is the King of the Earth, the last king whose rule is now underway over the whole planet with governments.

DID YOU KNOW?

If we say we will crown Him king when we get to heaven, we are denying His monarchy now. He has defeated the rulers of the world and is the eternal King. All rulers on the earth are under His authority and will answer to Him for their evil regimes and laws.

Paul wrote to the Corinthians about the resurrection and kingdom in his first epistle.

> Then cometh the end, when he shall have delivered up the kingdom to God, even the father; when he shall have put down all rule and all authority and power. For he must reign, till he hath put all enemies under his feet. The last enemy that shall be destroyed is death. For he hath put all things under his feet. But when he

61

saith all things are put under him, it is manifest that he is accepted, which did put all things under him. And when all things shall be subdued unto him, then shall the son also himself be subject unto him that put all things under him, that God may be all in all. (1 Corinthians 15:24–28)

God's initial intention was to have a kingdom of earthly beings, but before that kingdom could develop, Adam gave it to Satan. God would still have His kingdom of holy people to live on the earth as ordained from the first day man was created, and under Satan's nose, He did just that, first with the Law and now with grace. "The mystery of God should be finished as he hath declared to his servants and prophets" (Revelation 10:7).

CHAPTER 11

Casting Out Satan

Now, SOME WOULD RATHER have the rapture, seven years of great tribulation, a battle with the Devil, and finally Christ's bondage of Satan and thousand-year reign on earth sometime in the future. He then will release Satan to destroy the city of God and His saints yet another time—the very thing the saints were taken in the rapture before the great tribulation to prevent. This is premillennial doctrine.

The Scripture states,

> Cast him into the bottomless pit, and shut him up, and set a seal upon him, *that he should deceive the nations no more, till the thousand years should be fulfilled:* and after that he must be loosed a little season. (Revelation 20:3)

Note that the emphasized section in this Scripture is the reason Satan was to be let loose after the thousand years were completed. Who do you think the Devil is being let loose on, the resurrected saints from the days of the Law? No! They are already immortal. He would be on the earthly Christians like a duck on a june bug, consuming them with terror. When we think about the binding of Satan, think about it as Peter wrote: "For if God spared not the angels that sinned, but cast them down to hell, and delivered them into chains of darkness, to be reserved into judgment" (2 Peter 2:4). Consider also Jude 6: "And the angels which kept not their first estate, but left their own habitation, he hath reserved in everlasting chains of darkness unto the judgment of the great day."

When Christ's reign is complete, everyone who died lost or is still living wickedly will be cast into the lake of fire and brimstone, where the beast and false prophet are. Satan's spirit will enter the lake of fire too, for it is in the flesh of those wicked lost souls and will be forever, never to escape. The believer will inherit heaven—no Devil there, praise God. The judgment is happening now and is called the white throne judgment, for when we are forgiven of our sins, we pass before the judgment seat of Christ. If we're accepted, we receive life; if we're rejected, we receive death. Why? The flesh is evil and satanic and was duty-bound by the Law of Moses and released from the Law by grace, free to be resurrected under Christ's salvation. Satan's nature has been in the dark hearts of earthlings since he fell. No matter where our mortal bodies are, they will sin, because they are flesh with sinful natures—unless Christ changes their hearts. The flesh is like its father, Satan (John 8:44), and will do evil against the kingdom of God. If we think about God's spirit within us, Satan's is the same. Spirits must have a body to occupy and use, somewhat similar to God's use of our bodies to accomplish His work. Wicked spirits have no rest without a body.

Darkness binds Satan like it does the lost. Forever he will remain bound by that darkness. The same darkness engulfed the human race, but the whole time the Law was in force, the children of God walked in light, because they did not obey the flesh, and sin. Christ defeated

Satan's hold on the inhabitants of the earth by grace. The lost are still bound by Satan's sinful nature; they live only by the law of the land, which when they break, they are against Christ Jesus, the earth's ruler. Satan's influence is still active in the hearts of sinful men, because mankind is flesh, and the flesh is sinful. We cannot stop sinning unless we have a power stronger than our flesh. Even under an iron rule with Satan bound in chains and sealed in a bottomless pit, his spirit is free, and we will continue to sin without grace. As long as we are in these fleshly bodies, the flesh can cause us to fall. Only the power of God can save us. Satan's influence is in the flesh of all earthlings. The world was not lawless before the Law was instituted, for rulers made laws to keep their kingdoms intact. Men lived according to their knowledge of good and evil and became more lawless as time passed because their evil nature overpowered their good nature, and after the fall, they could have never done any good without the spirit of God breathed into Adam at creation. People did not know they were sinful until the Law revealed their flesh to be sinful. The Law of God caused men to recognize sin, and Law put them to death if they broke it.

Christ is the end of the Law, Romans 10; 4 and we were freed from the Law and put under grace through faith. Grace controls our flesh, because grace is stronger than the Law and our flesh, which is under the power of Satan. As long as men are in fleshly bodies, they will sin—unless they accept Christ as their Savior. The spirit of God in Christians is what restrains the evil power of the lost! Thank God for us!

DID YOU KNOW?

We are resurrected already. Our eternal life starts the day we are translated into Christ's kingdom by new birth. We already live as new creatures on the earth with the heathens who are still guided by their fleshly bodies. Satan is still in the flesh of all unbelievers, but he can still deceive and devour whomever he may. This is an amazing analogy—the future kingdom men teach and the current one.

Premillennial scholars believe that the rapture saints in glorified bodies and those who make it through the great tribulation in fleshly bodies will live together in this New Jerusalem under the rule of Christ. It's quite odd that we live that way now, under grace!

Since men teach that Satan has no power to wreak havoc and disrupt peace if he is bound, we are to believe he has been loosed since the fall of Adam. I think it is safe to say that he was both loosed as well as bound, but the difference is that premillennial believers conclude there is a place where Satan is to be put away and cannot tempt humans while this period is in operation. Excuse me! What God revealed to me is that there is no place to lock Satan up where he has no influence, because a spirit cannot be shut up unless one is doomed to dwell in the hearts of humans, the dust of the earth, by his Creator. Only a power stronger than the flesh could stop Satan, and that was the restraining power of the Law first and then grace. If the flesh of man is bound, Satan is too. I believe his spirit has been constrained in the flesh of man since the fall by the law of men and then the Law of God. The Law of the Jews was still in effect until the temple and all Jerusalem was destroyed in AD 70. However, grace was also abounding at the same time in the hearts of believers saved through the preaching of the apostles. There are so many doctrines; it is hard to separate them all. I only know what God has taught me concerning those restraining times while the purpose and plan of salvation was in the making.

A LITTLE ABOUT SPIRITS

Men teach that God walked with man in the garden paradise and that Adam saw God. Well, this cannot be true, for God is Spirit, John 4: 24, and who can see a spirit? Scripture clearly states that no man has seen God and lived. "And he said, Thou canst not see my face: for there shall no man see me, and live" (Exodus 33:20). *We then can conclude that Adam never saw God either.*

God revealed to me that He walked and talked with Adam on a

daily basis in the person of his cherub, Lucifer; As mentioned earlier, I realized this while studying Abraham and the angels that came to visit him concerning the destruction of Sodom, where his nephew Lot was. God always sent angels to visit His people when His plans concerned them. It was the same with Abram.

God sent angels, which appeared to Abram as men—just as the cherub was sent to commune with Adam, going to and fro in the earth with instructions and results. So, when Adam was in the garden, Satan was too. When the word of God was delivered to man, Lucifer was the courier. He knew exactly what God told man, because he and God communed every day concerning His creation. There was no actual snake in the garden that talked and walked upright. The snake was Satan himself. Do you think for one minute Eve would have listened to one of the creatures talking? No! She would have known something was amiss. But since it was the guardian, she never gave it a thought. Any time we carry on a conversation with the Devil, we are headed for trouble, and he is always disguised. So we can see how the angels have been instrumental to God's creation all along.

So now I will provide you with a little more insight on the binding and loosing of Satan. He was in the flesh of Adam after the fall of man. When Noah was preparing the ark, he was there too. After the flood, he was there. When Jacob went down into Egypt, Satan went too. In Job 1:6 we have a conversation between God and Satan when the sons of God prepared themselves to meet God; Satan was there too, in the flesh of the believers. He was always with God's people. That is what his purpose was in the beginning, and what God ordains is fixed until time is abolished. But when the Law was drawn up, men realized who Satan was, putting the fear of death in them and a halt to his destructiveness, binding him tight as a mummy in the flesh of God's people. The Law restrained man's flesh so men could be taught about God and about the consequences of sin. If man sinned under the Law, the death penalty was enforced, but moreover, man was already dead with the second death facing him. So, the Law controlled man's will to sin and thus brought sin to a halt, and it continued to bind man until the promised Savior entered the world. The flesh is controlled by Satan's sinful influence, even when chains of darkness bind him. The Law bound the flesh of man, and when flesh is bound, Satan is too, because the Law was stronger than the flesh. Grace, however, is stronger than the Law.

Satan walked and talked with Adam, teaching him God's plan for his life, which he took from him, bringing death to him and his descendants through disobedience. Christ walked and talked with his disciples, teaching them about His new paradise, the New Jerusalem, and He gave life back to men through grace. Praise God forever! So after Christ's death and our salvation, we become just like Him, with power to overcome the flesh—just like the power the Law gave the Israelites, but without all its rituals.

Now, are we then to believe Satan can deceive us after we become immortal? God forbid! But the fleshly nations are a different story. The Bible says Eve was deceived, not Adam; he willingly sinned, for he heard what God said about that tree in the midst of the garden before Eve was created.

Revelation 20 states Satan will be let loose to deceive the nations once more. "Once more" means there must have been an earlier time when Satan deceived the nations. There was—when He deceived Eve, the mother of all living. The nation was in her womb, for God instructed Adam and Eve to multiply and replenish the earth (Genesis 1:28). The fullness of time (Galatians 4:4) was for all people, not just Jews, so deception was halted until the Savior could deliver the oracles of God for the redemption of His creation to the apostles.

Grace was first preached in Jerusalem by Christ, who taught it to the Jewish disciples, who in turn delivered the gospel to the lost tribes of Hebrew descendants and then to the rest of the world. I cannot understand why the premillennialists teach that the Jews have not preached the gospel but will carry the gospel during the tribulation. Do they not see the Jews have preached the gospel already?

He said unto them, Go ye into all the world, and preach the gospel to every creature. And they went forth, and preached everywhere, the Lord working with them, and confirming the word with signs following. Amen. (Mark 16:15,20)

The apostles did exactly what John the Baptist did—they foreran the ministry of Jesus, calling for repentance, for the kingdom of God was at hand. The disciples called for the entire world to repent. Jews went into the world, preaching the gospel of grace to prepare sinners, for the king was at hand. Today's biblical scholars say the Jew will carry the gospel during the great tribulation. Were the persecutions suffered by the Jewish nation during the destruction of Jerusalem not a great tribulation? And did the Jews carry the gospel then also?

About the loosing of Satan—during the lapse of time between the resurrection of Christ and the destruction of Jerusalem, Satan's spirit was loosed from the flesh of believers by grace, which allowed him to deceive and destroy. But Satan's spirit and Jesus' spirit cannot dwell in the same house. But if he is cast out of believers, where does he go? (Again, when the unclean spirit goes out, it looks for a house to dwell in (Matthew 12).) The little season arrived, if you will, and is why Christ did not ascend into heaven for forty days until the apostles knew He was very much alive. That bottomless pit was the Devil's fate until Christ's death, after which his spirit was cast out of the hearts of believers, free to devour whom he found empty. The lake of fire and brimstone is his fate, where the beast and the false prophet are. Remember, he still operates in the flesh of believers and sinners alike when they yield themselves to him (hence the deceiving of the nations), because our souls are still in fleshly bodies.

CHAPTER 12

Millennium or Kingdom

DID YOU KNOW?

ACCORDING TO PREMILLENNIAL TEACHING, **saints in their new bodies live with the heathens in their old bodies, and the saved remain restored or new creatures amid those lost souls in their still carnal bodies. Is this not a picture of the very same kind of kingdom men teach to be of the future? I submit that this a picture of God's kingdom now, established by His Son, Jesus.**

If there was a thousand-year period as taught, it had to have been during the time of the tribes of priests and kings carrying the Law of God in the old dispensation. Even Christ lived during that time. We are a kingdom of kings and priests too, ordained by God to carry the gospel of grace or oracles of salvation until the long-awaited King returns for His bride, God's children, and His Father's kingdom. The holy period of the first priest was replaced by the second, and all that's left for us to do is to tell the world about our coming king. It is amazing how the second child succeeded the first in biblical history—two Adams, two kingdoms, two restraining powers, two worlds, two spirits controlling the flesh, etc. Aren't you glad we are blessed by the second?

The Law could keep the Hebrews from committing sin, but the grave was another matter. The only way to overcome death, hell, and the grave is to defeat Satan—to reverse the curse. The Law did not do that; it only made men responsible for their sin and brought a death sentence if the Law was broken. When men die in their sin, they enter the second death. There had to be something stronger than the flesh of man to stop sin. The Law was. It was stronger than the flesh, teaching men how to overcome it. So the Law was more powerful than the flesh, saving men from the death caused by sin, but limited in that it could not raise them from the grave.

Now, during this Law period, God raised up His special people—the priest, prophets, and kings—to teach and enforce the Law. The do's and don'ts of the Law started with Moses and ended when Christ died. (Death reigned from Adam to Moses.) Grace resulted from Christ's work on Calvary, and grace is stronger than the flesh, the Law, and death. Grace is what Adam was under and fell from, and death is where he fell to. Christ's work restored us to God through grace, exactly to the place Adam was before he fell, by the rule of Christ over the earth that occurred when Satan lost the battle for supremacy to Jesus, the victor. This was the end of the world in John 13:31, and the power over mankind was moved to the kingdom of God, which is ruled from His seat in heaven where our King now sits. *Kingdom* is the right word, but it is neither millennial nor temporary, unless one uses the term of the Law days, for the Law was temporary, ending when Christ became the eternal King of the earth. Also, according to biblical events, from the time the Law was established until Christ's death and the temple destruction, a little over one thousand years—or a millennium—passed, the duration of the Law. But the Bible says the rest of the dead did not live again until the thousand years were finished. If the millennium and the thousand years are one and the same, then it has passed.

The kingdom God deployed on earth was to have its start in and with Adam, a nation of people dependent on the God of the universe, people with the power to subdue and build. This is why Satan has always been with man; together they were doing what was ordained. Satan, however, did not know he would become trapped in the flesh of mankind, praise God. Even after the fall, the ordained traits were still ensuing from their masters. Cain built a city. His sons built cities. Men have built and ruled ever since. Why? They were ordained to do that, just as the sun rises in the east and sets in the west every day. What God ordains is fixed until the day it is ordained to be abolished. His kingdom is eternal, grace is eternal, and we are eternal beings. Long live the King! The Law was temporary, and so was the millennium!

With grace, we do not need the letter of the Law to know right from wrong, for it is engraved on the tables of our hearts of flesh from the first day of our new birth. Gone are the hearts of stone. We become just like Christ when we accept salvation. That is the first day of the rest of our lives. Grace is for the free children; the Law is for the enslaved.

When Christ was born, He was exactly like us in that He was flesh and bone and spirit. The blood was the only difference. Ours was full of sin, passed on from Adam, full of disease and death. Christ, on the other hand, was fathered by God with holy blood flowing through His veins. He was exactly like Adam before the fall. There was no knowledge of sin in Him. He was also like Adam when the tempter came and tried the same trick of deception on Him, but Christians cannot be deceived if they study and understand the oracles of God. If they sin, it is because they did not know the Word of God as they should, for Satan uses what is common to man to break his will, because the flesh is weak even after the new birth. Christ knew that He was King already and would be the earth's supreme ruler. Satan knew it too.

"And the lord commended the unjust steward, because he had done wisely: for the children of this world are in their generation wiser than the children of light" (Luke 16:8). There is a truth here. If we do not learn the ways of God, it will be easier to fall.

When the Spirit of God draws a sinner to repentance, Satan may tell that recipient of eternal life that he still has plenty of time to be converted or that he is not already converted, and in all probability Satan has plenty of time to have him killed. Satan cannot kill us, because Adam did not have power over other humans to that extent. So Satan causes men to murder, like he did with Cain. Satan lies every time he speaks, and his lies cheat us out of what we already have. To Satan, the only good Christian is a dead Christian. Kill the shepherd; scatter the sheep. Kill the king; capture the city. We Christians are the city of God, full of grace and glory.

With grace instituted, Christ fulfilled the Law and thus freed mankind at His death. Grace restored us as sons to the Father, but it loosed Satan's sinful influence to deceive us like he did Eve. No, God is not uncaring or mean. He restores us to sons made exactly like Christ, filled with His Spirit and life. We have to do the overcoming and must learn obedience. We must learn to listen to the Father. Only those who overcome this world will overcome Satan, and only those who do so will enter heaven. This is what grace brings to us—overcoming power! We saw earlier how Satan works. We must learn who we are in Christ and learn how to obey and communicate with God. Christ has complete rule of the earth, and thanks to Him, we can overcome the Devil too, because we are Christ like.

If men could reverse their way of thinking about the millennium and put it in the order as described here, they could see how urgent it is to preach that the King is coming instead of the kingdom. We are the city where God dwells. Nowhere in the Epistles does it teach that the kingdom is coming. Jesus and John the Baptist both preached to prepare for the kingdom that was at hand. The Epistles taught that the King is coming, and He, my friend, *will come* to take us with Him and deliver us, the finished kingdom, to God.

> Then cometh the end, when he shall have delivered up
> the kingdom to God, even the Father; when he shall

have put down all rule and all authority and power. For he must reign, till he hath put all enemies under His feet. The last enemy that shall be destroyed is death. For he hath put all things under his feet. But when he saith all things are put under him, it is manifest that he is accepted, which did put all things under him. And when all things shall be subdued unto him, then shall the Son also himself become subject onto him that put all things under him, that God may be all in all. (1 Corinthians 15:24–28)

The last enemy to be destroyed will be death, which will occur when the last sinner's satanic spirit is cast into the lake of fire, the second death. Once that happens, Satan will be destroyed, because his spirit and power on earth will be over. The resurrection destroys death, which is why we must be born again. The first resurrection isn't over yet! It began when Christ rose and will end when the kingdom is delivered to the Father at the last trump, the trump of assembly (Numbers 10:2). There is no second resurrection, just second (and last) coming.

Did You Know?

The Law finished the work it was created to do by preserving those who feared and honored it and died upholding it. By doing so, the grave was not the end of life, but the beginning of eternal life after Christ's resurrection, since its hold on its recipients was destroyed.

CHAPTER 13

What about the New Jerusalem?

Did You Know?

Concerning these Scriptures, we are the city or kingdom of God. In us He dwells, moves, and has His being. We are the city adorned as a bride. We are the bride adorned as a city, the city of God.

In the book of Revelation, we read the description of the holy city men say we will dwell in after the rapture—but is it the city where we will dwell or the city where God dwells? Have you read theses Scriptures closely enough to understand that it is not a literal city, but a bride? Let us look at them and it.

And I saw a new heaven and a new earth: for the first heaven and earth were passed away; (for they drowned in the flood) and there was no more sea. [Not seas as in oceans, but ungodly men in a wild and restless condition.] And I John saw the holy city, New Jerusalem, coming down from God out of heaven, prepared as a bride adorned for her husband. And I heard a great voice out of heaven saying,

Behold, the tabernacle of God is with men, and he will dwell with them, and they shall be his people, and God himself shall be with them, and be their God. And God shall wipe away all tears from their eyes; and there shall be no more death, neither sorrow, nor crying, neither shall there be any more pain: for the former things are passed away. And he that sat upon the throne said, Behold, I make all things new. And he said unto me, write: for these words are true and faithful…. And there came unto me one of the seven angels which had the seven vials full of the seven last plagues, and talked with me, saying, Come hither, I will shew thee the bride, the Lamb's wife. And he carried me away in the spirit to a great and high mountain, and shewed me that great city, the holy Jerusalem, descending out of heaven from God, having the glory of God: and her light was like unto a stone most precious, even like a jasper stone, clear as crystal…. Blessed are they that do his commandments, that they may have right to the tree of life, and may enter in through the gates into the city: for without are dogs, and sorcerers, and whoremongers, and murders, and idolaters, and whosoever loveth and maketh a lie. (Revelation 21:1–5,9–11; 22:14–15)

Do you believe the holy city Jerusalem described here houses us safe inside? In millennial teaching, the saints in glorified bodies live together with those from tribulation in bodies of flesh while Satan is bound. If so, what are sinners doing outside? Here, God is describing the bride, of whom we are, and issues an invitation in Revelation 22:17 to those on the outside:

> The Spirit and the bride say, come, and let them that heareth say, Come. And let him that is athirst come. And whosoever will, let him take the water of life freely.

If we, the glorified saints, are safe inside an eternal city, why is the Spirit giving an invitation to those sinners on the outside—especially when we've been taught that the Holy Spirit will be taken from the earth during the great tribulation? Well, from what Scripture tells me, no one can be saved unless the Spirit of God draws him, and God is that Spirit. Hey, we are not home yet!

Who is the bride inside the city if sinners are on the outside? The Old Testament saints raised in Matthew 27 with Christ? No, it is we, the New Jerusalem still on earth. We are the city of God preparing for her husband. If this is the thousand-year kingdom and the end of the world, has passed or is coming to pass, how can there be an invitation to lost souls? Indeed, how can there even be lost souls when these city dwellers are supposed to be in glorified bodies from the rapture, and some still in fleshly bodies after overcoming Satan during the tribulation?

The description of the city given by John is the kingdom in the making described also in 2 Corinthians 5:17: "Therefore if any man be in Christ, he is a new creature: old things are passed away; behold, all things are become new, *even the heavens and the earth*."

We have been restored to sons as Adam was before the fall, when he dwelled in a perfect place with God where no evil was known. The difference for us is that when these old bodies die, they will die perfected to be raised perfect. In other words, we must be converted by Christ and won away from Satan before these fleshly bodies die, so the second death can have no hold on us.

Did You Know?

Every person on earth is saved already. It was a done deal when Christ died, and all we have to do is believe to become new creatures. Christ died one time for everyone—past, present, and future. Everything has been done except the believing. Once that happens, the heart is changed, and we become sinless. Christ died once for all.

> And almost all things are by the law purged with blood, and without the shedding of blood there is no remission. It was therefore necessary that the patterns of things in heaven should be purified with these, but the heavenly things themselves with better sacrifices than these. For

Christ is not entered into the holy places made with hands, which are the figures of the true; but into heaven itself, now to appear in the presence of God for us: Nor yet that he should offer himself often, as the high priest entereth into the holy place every year with blood of others. For then must he often have suffered since the foundation of the world: but now in the end of the world hath he appeared to put away sin by the sacrifice of himself. And it is appointed unto men once to die, but after this the judgment. So Christ was once offered to bear the sins of many, and onto them that look for him shall he appear the second time without sin unto salvation. (Hebrews 9:22–28)

The book of Romans tells us in chapter 8 that we are passed from condemnation into eternal life through Christ. How? By doing the same exact thing the Law required: obeying. In another Scripture we are warned about not believing and being condemned already (John 3:18). So we are therefore judged worthy or unworthy of eternal life the instant we accept or refuse the options delivered to us by the apostles. After we are raised from the grave, we are separated and marched off to our eternal destination, and then the kingdom of God will be turned over to the Father while the unbelievers are destroyed, facing the same fate as the Devil and his angels.

For the time is come that judgment must first begin at the house of God: and if it first begins at us, what shall the end be of them that obey not the gospel of God? (1 Peter 4:17)

Look now at Hebrews 10:12,14:

But this man, after he had offered one sacrifice for sins forever, sat down on the right hand of God…. For by

one offering he hath perfected forever them that are
sanctified.

His blood covered the whole world. The saving work was done at
one time for every man, forever, and neither He nor we, the Christians,
can die again.

Notice also that He died in the end of the world! If it was the end
of the world then, what are we expecting when He comes again? Life?
Death? War? Armageddon? Desire peace, for He said, "The kingdom
of God is not meat and drink; but righteousness, and peace, and joy in
the Holy Ghost" (Romans 14:17).

The world as was known to the Jews was destroyed when Christ put
down Satan. Rome was no longer in power, and Israel did not come
into power, as the Jews thought would happen when the Messiah came.
It was the end of world rule when He died, and the eternal kingdom
was offered to the gentile. It will be the end of the world for you when
you die, unless you are saved. If we are not ready to meet him face to
face when the physical death of the body takes place, we will be raised
corruptible, and the lake of fire will become our abode with Satan
forevermore. The end of the world meant no more world rule. All these
kings, dictators, prime ministers, etc. who think the kingdoms they
control are theirs probably don't know that a one world ruler is already
ruling—from heaven.

A little information on the judgment may be in order here. If and
when we are born again, we are passed from judgment unto salvation.
We are judged when we ask Christ to come into our hearts. If we are
truly repentant, we pass from judgment into our eternal life the instant
we accept Him as Savior. Even those who reject Him will be judged at
the moment they refuse Him. This is the judgment of the white throne,
if you will. He will separate us on the final day, because He knows full
well who is His and who is not, for we all have, saved or rejected, passed
through the judgment seat of Christ on our way to salvation or eternal
death (Romans 8:1).

Chapter 14

Kingdom? Where?

DOES IT REALLY MATTER where the kingdom is? Since I was a child I have heard of a heaven. "In the sky" was the answer I was given. It seems to fit now that I have read the following Scripture telling me that His kingdom is not of this world, but is a heavenly kingdom on earth, as Ephesians 2:6 reveals. And is where we, His body, sit now. Jerusalem was the capital of Israel and the seat of David. The temple of God was built there to entice the Hebrews to worship as the other kingdoms had done. The destruction of Jerusalem by Satan was predicted as true prophecy, and the city was left desolate, never to rule again. That opportunity was lost when the Jews defied Jesus and put Him to death.

> Jesus answered, My kingdom is not of this world: if my kingdom were of this world, then would my servants fight, that I should not be delivered to the Jews: but now is my kingdom not from hence. (John 18:36)

Godly men will build no temple in Jerusalem for worship there in the future, because we are the temple of God. However, those believing themselves chosen to build a temple may attempt to; these people believe a lie and will be damned.

In the days of the kings, servants of the kings fought to keep their kingdoms. Saul's was such a kingdom. He knew David was the appointed king, and he knew why he lost the kingdom to David, but he did not give it up without a fight. (Sounds like the Devil!) Talk about ashamed—everyone would know he failed miserably if his sons did not succeed him to the throne. So Saul fought to stop David's appointment to that seat just as the Jewish priest fought to keep Christ off the throne. Saul forgot he was God's servant, as well as the citizens that made up the province he ruled. He liked the praise of the people and was more Afraid of losing it and his kingdom than obeying God. His son would not succeed him, and he was as good as dead.

We forget—or maybe are just not aware—that we are the product of our fathers. We never die as long as the name lives on. This explains the Scripture calling Abraham "as good as dead", therefore sprang there even of one, and him as good as dead, so many as the stars of the sky in multitude, and as the sand which is by the sea innumerable (Hebrews 11:12) and compares the scripture with God as our Father. Abraham had no heir. Without offspring, his race would be extinct, just as many of our species are today. Isaac was his cure from death just as Christ is ours.

People are the kingdom. When a king rules, it is over people, although he has complete say in every matter concerning that realm. We have been the kingdom all along, Jew and Greek alike, just as it was supposed to be when God said to replenish and multiply. That is what John saw. Needless to say, we were indescribable! He saw the city where God dwells.

CHAPTER 15

A Few Bugs in the Rapture

THINK ABOUT WHAT YOU have heard about the many phases of the second coming of Christ. Some teach that Christ will come four or even five more times. These comings are called phases. Let's see—He has been here as the Son of Man (one), He is coming to rapture us (two) and then again after tribulation to bind Satan and establish the millennial kingdom (three), He is coming again to release Satan during the little season when he is released from the bottomless pit (four), and He will make His final appearance in judgment (five). If we miss the first, we just need to hold on. We still have a chance, because there is a few more times He must appear—and most assuredly, we will see His final coming.

These phases were what convinced me to get this word out. I heard a Christian woman say after a Bible study about the rapture and the phases of Christ's comings that she was sure glad she had another chance to make it if she missed the rapture. I don't want to miss heaven, so I want to go in the first load. It is also taught that the saints who are blessed enough to participate in the rapture before tribulation go straight to the marriage supper of the Lamb. If that is true, are those who make it through the seven years of tribulation and then through the millennial kingdom, as taught, His bride also? Since they missed the marriage supper, could they be called His concubines? Better hope we go in the first batch!

What's most astonishing is that we believe the same thing we criticized the Jews for when Christ came in the flesh. They were looking for a fighting king to rule the earth. Some denominations are also looking for a fighting king to rule the Earth. Are we any different from them? They had all the signs in place. He was born of the right lineage and was a prophet, priest, and king but was cast away because he was not a fighting king. Men want and teach the same thing this day and time and will not have it any other way.

Not many people believe He is king now and executes power over the earth, that He defeated Satan and took the world back, or that He sits on the throne in the eternal heaven where He now reigns. They would rather have a king that comes to earth, fights the earthlings and Satan, takes the city of Jerusalem, and establishes a kingdom—one, by the way, that is not eternal.

Revelation 20 states that Satan will be released to deceive the nations once more after the thousand years are finished, waging a battle that causes fire to fall on him and his cohorts, destroying them. Then, when the great white throne and God are revealed, the heavens and earth flee, and no place for them will be found. Is not this a temporary city? Can we eternal beings, knowing that Satan will unleash his cohorts on us again for a little season, call this peace? I do not believe anyone living in such a time as that could have peace.

If we are in fleshly bodies, unregenerate or not, this flesh is going to give us combat whether Satan is bound or not. Look at the battle we fight now, with Jesus on the inside!

It is far better to believe that the Law bound Satan, grace released him, and grace will cause us to overcome the wiles of the flesh until the second and final coming of the King. The king is dead; long live the King!

CHAPTER 16

The Last Day

IN THE DAYS OF yore, the kings of the earth ruled the whole earth, long ago in the East. The influences of the last empire of earthly rule are still felt today. The greatest and swiftest was the warrior king named Alexander of Macedon, whose fighting pose had never before been seen, for he could figure out how to make a hole in an army's defense and go right in, swallowing up whole kingdoms. His swiftness and might were unsurpassed by any before him or after, and the effect of his expertise is still a power today. Alexander readied the world for history's greatest king. Alexander enter the world theater with an influence that has captivated millions, not only with fighting strategies, but also with the knowledge of peace and love, which causes men to put down their weapons and pick up a book of history, decoding and implementing his doctrine to save and not kill. He also made Greek the official and only language of his empire, undoing the confusion at God's dispersion of the people at the Tower of Babel and gathering them together again in Jerusalem with a weapon called language. Pentecost!

To understand what is meant here is to understand what has been before. This world had a king named Satan, whose cunning is in the flesh of all his subjects. They follow him and do not even know they are in bondage because he lets them be like him, enjoying what they believe to be freedom. In the beginning he used sleight of words to overpower Adam and take his kingdom, and when Adam's eyes were opened, it was too late. The sad truth is that God has to open our spiritual eyes before we can see the Devil; we must be awake and alert at all times to overcome. Humanity has been under the influence of Satan's evil power ever since the fall of man with only one way out from under it, and that power was offered two thousand years ago by a man whose wisdom overthrew the Enemy in the same way it was used on the first man at the beginning of the world.

This man was the Messiah, the coming King prophesized throughout history by men of God anointed to write and tell the story of the demise of the Evil One. John 12:31 tells the story, and it was done under the noses of the world leaders (Acts 4:26–28) who thought that an earthly fighting king would take over and rule their world. Christ did not do that—He let them keep their kingdoms, power, and glory—but because men do not understand the Word of God, they believe that a great king on a white horse will come swooping down to usher in a futuristic Davidic kingdom with Jerusalem as its capital. Talk about being under the noses of world leaders! He is doing it again, and He said little children could understand it. After just three and a half years, it was a done deal, and leading biblical scholars still don't know what happened. On top of all that, the scholars have come up with the wrong conclusion concerning the end of the world as we know it and are teaching damnable doctrines that cause the human race to look for another king who will rule the world—and he is called the Antichrist.

A man named John had a vision about the takeover of the world by the King of Glory. What he saw was symbolic, and he became amazed and fainted. God told him to write what he saw in a book and send it to the seven churches in Asia. Why these churches? It was because these churches sat in the slime pits of evil, and Jerusalem would fall to Titus, resulting in the destruction of any churches there. Asia would surely hear about the churches in Jerusalem, and fear could cause them to give up (Luke 21:20; Revelation 20:9). What John was revealing to the churches in Asia was the fall of Rome, and they would endure if they didn't faint, so letters were sent to secure their hearts and minds. World church leaders are teaching their people about the destruction of churches when they should be teaching that God will not let Christians endure anything they cannot conquer.

As I studied the Scriptures, God revealed to me that another John, the Baptist, needed to know if the one whose shoe latchets he was not worthy to touch, the one whom he preached about, was the coming King. John needed to understand the same thing, so God showed him. We are never in the dark concerning the future, because God still has a few forerunners paving the way, and they let the world know about the future to enlighten them and give them hope.

We have teachers out there today who use the Word of God to deceive poor, unlearned souls, such as Bible toters. They write book after book, so some will buy, read, and tote them to learn all about the secrets of the end times, making the authors millionaires. Isn't that a shame? It was the same with me until the day I got so confused that I threw up my hands and made a profound statement that changed my whole life, as well as my understanding concerning Scripture. Here are those words: *"There has to be one simple truth."* I found it when I stopped spending hard-earned money on books to help me understand the Bible when I had the one who inspired men to write it to teach me all I needed to know.

Is that like you today? Are you reading all the books you can find about the end of time? Stop right there and put them away until you read the truth, which can and will set you free.

Now, let me use the major verse in Scripture that has been misused. It is "on the Lord's Day," as John was in when he had his vision, Rev. 1:10. This word, *day*, is spelled in the Greek, *kuriakos*, as an adjective, is the day of his manifested judgment on the world, meaning "last day."[3] John 12:23 states, "Jesus answered them, saying, The hour is come, that the Son of man should be glorified." Read through verse thirty-two, but notice thirty-one: "Now is the judgment of this world: now shall the prince of this world be cast out." *This is exactly what Jesus means in John's gospel about the end of the world,* meaning that earthly rule was over—or, better still, that this was the last *day* that men would rule on earth! The kingdom of God was taking over the earth and its people, defeating Satan's spirit and stopping sin.

We read about the church, the woman clothed with the sun, giving birth while the devil stood before her to destroy her child. We read about the bowls, seals, and trumpets, and the wrath of Him who sits the throne visiting those rulers who were supposed to rule justly. John's letter was meant to encourage the churches and to let them know that God did not abandon them and that even if their pastors were far removed from them, as John was, God was ever near. They read about the words of Jesus concerning the fall of Jerusalem and the fall of Rome, which were an encouragement, for I know within reason that His words were taught to them. The punishment meted out according to the unjust treatment of God's people was just. After all, he is the King of the earth and can inflict justice, no matter how severe it seems to be. How far into the future the book reaches I do not know, but I do know the seven churches needed to know what lay ahead for them, or else they could not have survived and more than likely would have taken that mark of allegiance against Christ. The mark of allegiance is working in this evil time too, and poor souls are falling for damnable doctrines and away from the true one. We too may do the same if we faint from watching the slaughter of our preachers.

In Revelation, John tells about the price of food. In Jerusalem, the people would have given all they had to buy a morsel of bread, and Larry Norman wrote a song about that subject, with one lyric stating, "a piece

---

3   W. E. Vine, *Vine's Complete Expository Dictionary of Old and New Testament Words* (Nashville: Thomas Nelson, 1996) 146. 1

of bread could buy a bag of gold."[4] Titus had Jerusalem surrounded for three and a half years. No one entered the city or left it. All those who would not listen to the words of the apostles were destroyed with it, and the only ones to escape were those warned about it being surrounded by armies. The citizens of Jerusalem actually ate their children and maybe their neighbors' children because they ran out of food. Some may have killed themselves—and all of this because they did not believe Jesus' words.

John saw the perfect church—the New Jerusalem, the Holy City—and revealed that to his followers. He told them about the Tree of Life, the living water, and the golden streets and throne. He told them that even if they died, life would return to them in perfection if they didn't faint.

This is what we need to know. That wrath is for the unjust, and if God kept the Israelites through the Red Sea, the three Hebrew children in the fiery furnace, Noah through the flood, and the New Testament church when Jerusalem fell, He can keep us as promised, and when Christ delivers the kingdom to God the Father, the rest for His people will begin. Amen!

---

4   Larry Norman, "I Wish We'd All Been Ready" (New York: Beechwood Music Corporation/J. C. Love, 1978).

In Closing

It is really amazing that the premillennial teaching is quite correct, just in the wrong time frame. Men theorize that Satan has been free to roam the earth, doing in every Christian who would obey him. Satan's spirit has been in the flesh of every human, either by the Law of God or by the law of the land, excepting the elect, bound by the Law first and then by grace. We were all children of darkness until the love of God filled us with light. The problem with humans is that we are by nature rebellious, and if men believe a lie, they will be damned. How many lies are found in the premillennial teaching? The first lie is that we haven't crowned Christ King yet. The next is that we have second chances. Another is that Christ will come in secret. (The Scriptures declare that every eye shall see him when He comes, and the nations of the earth shall tremble.) Another misconception is that we will live with unsaved fleshly humans after we're made immortal. The untruths go on and on, and we believe them all. And how many will surely be unprepared is anyone's guess.

God revealed to me that Revelation is a summary of the kingdom of God—the people, the priests, the kings, and the prophets He raised up to tell the story of the events that would deliver the just and destroy the wicked. Study what you have read herein, and let God make you aware of the future of the church for you and your love ones.

Lord, save us from the wiles of our flesh, which sins. Amen.

END